100852

REFORMATION AND SOCIETY
IN
SIXTEENTH-
CENTURY
EUROPE

REFORMATION
AND SOCIETY

IN

SIXTEENTH-CENTURY EUROPE

A. G. DICKENS

HARCOURT, BRACE & WORLD, INC.

*To Kathleen and Colin Kain
in friendship*

First American Edition 1966
Reprinted 1970

Library of Congress Catalog Number: 66-19863

PRINTED IN GREAT BRITAIN BY JARROLD AND SONS LTD NORWICH

CONTENTS

PREFACE

With the present essay I attempt a concise but balanced and human account of the Reformation in its social, political and intellectual setting. So far as my knowledge extends, I have sought to incorporate recent research and analysis, but publication continues on so great a scale and in so many places, that no one student can hope to keep abreast of every specialist advance, or even to remain guiltless of demonstrable errors. Brevity being the order of the day, many topics must be suggested rather than developed, yet the book will have served its main purpose if it reveals something of the amazing diversity and depth of the changes sweeping Europe at the moment when her culture was beginning effectively to expand and to reshape the destinies of the whole human race.

The simplest essay on such a theme leaves one with debts to living scholars far too numerous to be recorded in a preface or even in a reading-list like the one appended to the present book. I am grateful to three generous friends who read the whole typescript and suggested a number of modifications. One is my former colleague at Hull, James Atkinson, whose scholarship and profound experience of Luther I have found so inspiring over the years. Another is Edmund Fryde, who often places at my disposal the fruits of his far-ranging and cosmopolitan studies. The third is my colleague at King's, Patrick Collinson, alongside whom it is a rare privilege to study and to teach. In addition I must thank several other friends who sent me criticism and advice, books and offprints at crucial moments: Geoffrey Elton, H. R. Trevor-Roper, Gordon Rupp, G. R. Potter, Geoffrey Barraclough and C. W. Dugmore. Again, I received all possible help from my publishers, especially from Oliver Benn and Richard Howard: to the specialized knowledge and hard effort of the latter the credit for the illustrations remains very largely due.

A. G. DICKENS

King's College, London
September 1965

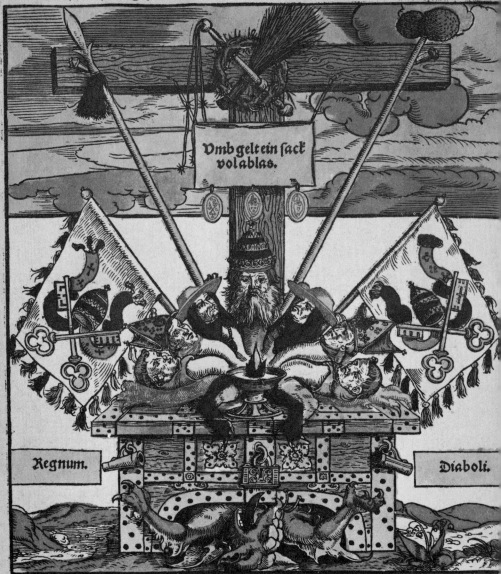

Vmb gelt ein sack vol ablas.

Regnum.

Diaboli.

1 'The Seven-Headed Papal Revelation'. Several streams of dissent have found their way into this German caricature of about 1530. The Papal beast (pope, cardinals, bishops, priests) is adapted from *Revelation*. Contemporary malpractice is cruelly marked out by the use of the cross, on which the bull of indulgence was customarily hung, to support, as well, the instruments of Christ's tormentors; the bull itself is made a purse into which money is to be 'thrown'. The chest is another property of the indulgence-sellers; the Devil is seen emerging from beneath it

I HERESY AND ANTICLERICALISM

By historians of religion the sixteenth century is regarded as an age of instability, of division and dissolution, the age when Europe saw the end of a united Christendom. Yet this crisis might also be envisaged as the final link in a whole chain of interlocking crises. The profound and complex tensions of the medieval centuries had in ever-increasing measure embraced the Catholic Church. Some of these tensions seem endemic to medieval civilization, while others arose in consequence of its decline. A military, a violent society, still by no means remote from the day of wandering war-bands, had never ceased to writhe in the grasp of religious and juridical ideals. Princes waged unremitting conflict with each other, with their own vassals, with the rising urban communities, with emperors, popes and prelates. The amoral elements in the code of chivalry contended against the biblical ethic, canon law against both the laws of states and the practice of merchants. Aristotelian scholasticism was forced to join issue first with Averroism and then with Nominalism; the tenacious pagan-classical tradition drew some men away from ascetic and pietist courses. Within and around the Church itself heresies rose and fell, while the mystical approach to religion found little in common with the rationalists of the universities and still less with the papal and episcopal administrators. The Church never ceased to attract potential saints, yet to climbers it offered easier, more glittering rewards than did secular careers and therein lay its deadliest peril.

During the fourteenth and fifteenth centuries both military and economic feudalism made way for less stable relationships, while the cities assumed those more vital rôles in the political and social life of nations which were to become so significant for the Protestant Reformation. Meantime the Papacy experienced at the hands of the

9

nation-states pressures even more acute than those formerly exerted by the Holy Roman Emperors. After a long absence from Italy spent at Avignon, it suffered division between rival popes, each backed by a group of European powers. It finally emerged from the hazards of the Conciliar movement with its spiritual powers unfettered by constitutional safeguards, its administration largely unreformed, its independence from secular manipulators still far from guaranteed. In short, we are witnessing no sudden leap from a calm and static medieval world into a dynamic sixteenth century. No doubt there are still those who see in medieval Europe a shining crusader crowned by feudal kingship, brandishing the sword of chivalry, obedient to the voice of St Peter, and protected by the exquisitely jointed armour of Thomist rationalism. But such deluded romantics should study the Fourth Crusade, the Albigenses, Emperor Frederick II, Philip IV of France and Boniface VIII, the Spiritual Franciscans, the Babylonian Captivity, the Council of Constance. Above all they should explore the social and intellectual turmoil of the fourteenth century, when already the weakened structure of Christendom seemed in danger of total collapse.

Nevertheless, some of these medieval tensions had been creative as well as destructive. Many were but regional in scope or limited in duration. Millions of orthodox men and women lived out their short life-spans in a seemingly immutable setting. Only here and there in the long story of medieval Europe did circumstances threaten to destroy public regard for papal and priestly authority, to create permanent doctrinal divisions or rival theories of salvation.

2 The peasant is made celebrant in an over-turned church, while priest and monk are set at the plough: wood-cut from Joseph Grünbeck's *Spiegel*, 'A mirror of natural, celestial and prophetic visions of all miseries' to come (Nuremberg, 1508)

After the apparent rout of the fourteenth century came the apparent rally of the fifteenth. Only during the first half of the sixteenth were the old tensions so heightened by new ones that they decisively tore the great gothic edifice apart. Then for a time it seemed that Catholicism might survive only in parts of Italy and in the Iberian Peninsula. Yet no less dramatically came the eleventh-hour revival, whereby the Church of Rome recovered or retained the allegiance of more than half the broken continent.

In the vastness of its setting, the profusion of its scenes, the fascination of its characters, the complexity of its emotions and ideas, our theme deserves a literary canvas as huge as that of *War and Peace* or of *The Dynasts*. It should not be made narrowly to revolve around a few great figures. The banners of Luther and Zwingli were borne aloft on the shoulders of mighty social and political forces; within a decade both movements had soared far beyond any mere personal guidance. The Protestant Reformation cannot be dismissed as an adjustment of relations between sovereigns and churches; it achieved its great historical importance just because it cut so deeply into society, because it brought even the common men of Europe to the barricades of religious revolution. Whatever the stature of its titans, a turmoil so widespread and so profound as this could not have arisen through any such simple agents. A flaming brand thrown into a heap of wet straw will hardly cause a smouldering. To explain the astonishing swiftness of the conflagration which followed Luther's defiance, we must begin by describing the climatic conditions which had made the straw of European society as dry as tinder.

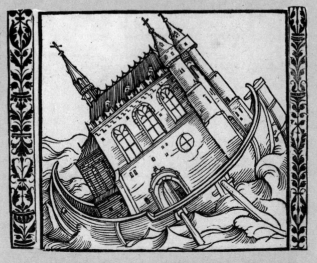

3 By the end of the fifteenth century, prophetic books such as Johann Lichtenberger's *Prenostication* (1497) were foretelling the wreck of the Church

During the half-century before the rise of Luther organized heresy can hardly have seemed to presage immediate cataclysms. Apart from a number of small and surreptitious sects, three major heretical movements existed in Europe: those of the Hussites in Bohemia and Moravia, the Lollards in England, and the Waldensians or Vaudois chiefly seated in the valleys of Savoy and Piedmont. Their beliefs had much in common, and all three were destined to establish interesting relationships with the coming Protestant Reformation. The Hussites had captured most attention, since by spectacular revolt the whole Czech people had asserted both its national and its religious identity. In terms of heretical belief this movement might be dubbed conservative. Most of the teachings of John Huss (c. 1369–1415) derived from Wycliffe, but the claims of the moderate majority of the Hussites centred around the principle of Utraquism: communion for the laity under the species of wine (confined by Catholic usage to the clergy) as well as under that of bread. Yet behind this apparently simple demand, there lurked the will to subordinate papal and Conciliar authority to that of the Bible. On this basic issue the Bohemian heresy forms a true prelude to the Protestant Reformation.

Though guaranteed to the Bohemians in 1433 by the Compactata of Prague, Utraquism had never received papal or Conciliar confirmation and in 1462 it had been denounced as heretical by Pope Pius II. From its beginning the national uprising had been weakened by radicalism and secession. Though the left-wing Taborites had suffered defeat at Lipan in 1434, their programmes had been in large part assumed by the Bohemian Brethren, who disapproved of oaths, refused military service, disliked private property, renounced town-life and demanded a simple unworldly Christianity. From about 1494 to 1528 the leader of the Brethren was Luke of Prague, a thinker of some originality, who in part anticipated Luther's emphasis on justification by faith but retained a celibate priesthood and all seven sacraments. With a striking breadth of purpose, he also visited the Waldensians and maintained contacts with the Orthodox Church. The junction of the Bohemian Brethren with Lutheranism was not to be completed until 1542, when they accepted its views on justification and consubstantiation but retained their peculiar disciplinary system of public and private confession. While Moravia remained their chief focus—hence their later title Moravian Brethren —many migrated to Poland, uniting there in 1555 with the Calvinists. Even in Luke's day they had not dwelt in unity, and about 1500 a group of rural rigorists called Amosites had separated from the main body. These Amosites, opposing the admission of townsmen and members of the privileged classes, wanted to see a society shaped around the Sermon on the Mount. They even included some radical extremists with anti-Trinitarian views.

4 Satan in a monk's gown (*left*): a striking image of early dissent from a fifteenth-century history of the Hussite movement

5 A century later, the illuminator of a song in praise of Huss, in the Bohemian *Gradual of Malá Strana* (1572), worked from a direct vision of the descent of the reform. *Above right:* John Wycliffe strikes a spark, Huss holds a candle, and Luther brandishes a torch. *Below:* Huss, wearing the traditional heretic's hat, adorned with devils, is burned at Constance (1415)

Luther realized the kinship between his teachings and those of the moderate Hussites; he welcomed both the conservatives and the Brethren as evangelical Christians. On the other hand, the Amosites naturally allied not with Luther but with the Anabaptists, some of whom soon afterwards migrated into Bohemia. In Moravia also there remained sectarians of fifteenth-century origin, who developed similar affinities with Anabaptism. Before Lutheranism arrived the situation in Bohemia-Moravia had thus already become complicated and nowhere more so than in Prague, where about a third of the inhabitants remained Catholic. While the Hussites gave comfort and support to the new German Reformation, they were too divided, too deeply immersed in their various native traditions to take a large share in the Protestant expansion. Their influence upon Poland and Hungary together with their general rôle in preparing central Europe for the Reformation have sometimes been exaggerated by Czech patriotism. Nevertheless, there lay some solid economic factors behind Bohemia's rôle in the world of ideas. This country has been styled 'the Nevada of Europe at the end of the Middle Ages'. Certainly the development of its mining industry attracted a large floating population of foreigners, many of whom subsequently went off and dispersed its religious and social ideas over the rest of central and eastern Europe.

As Hussitism had risen to dominance, the English Wycliffite or Lollard heresy had been driven underground. But from about 1485 we hear more and more of Lollard activities in England, and during the period 1500–30 the bishops waged intermittent persecution in their several dioceses. The Lollards still included a few merchants and substantial tradesmen of London, but their meetings consisted for the most part of artisans and peasants. Held together by wandering missionaries, they secretly studied Purvey's English translation of the Scriptures and other Lollard writings, all as yet in manuscript. Such congregations continued to flourish in London, Essex, Kent, Buckinghamshire and elsewhere, mainly in south-eastern England. Even in more conservative areas, anticlerical and antisacramental ideas apparently deriving from Lollardy often figure among charges made in the ecclesiastical courts. We know that heretics of Lollard

WILLIAM TINDALL

㉤The ne=
we Teſtament/dyly
gently coꝛrected and
compared with the
Greke by Wíllyam
Tíndale: and fyꝛeſ=
ſhed in the yere of ou
re Loꝛde God·
A. M. D. ꝼ. ꞃꞃꞏiiij.
in the moneth of
Nouember·

6 The First Revision (1534) of William Tyndale's *New Testament* in English:
title-page with facing portrait. Of the first edition of 1526, only two imperfect
copies survive

background welcomed Lutheranism; some engaged in the selling of
Tyndale's English *New Testament* (1526) and other printed works
by exiled English Lutherans. It is quite certain that Lollardy created
reception-areas for Lutheran and Zwinglian teachings, with which it
presently merged. Even as late as the reign of Mary Tudor the courts
prosecuted obscure heretics who still bore obvious marks of the older
Wycliffite tradition. Meanwhile English Protestant publicists had
furnished themselves with an English ancestry by printing several
old Wycliffite tractates. The Lollards had, it must be acknowledged,
anticipated many sixteenth-century Protestant positions. They had
exalted preaching above the sacraments, poured scorn upon transubstantiation and sought to place the vernacular Scriptures in the
hands of all men, learned and unlearned alike. They had denounced
clerical celibacy, confession, prayers for the dead, pilgrimages,
images, ecclesiastical wealth and the inordinate passion of the
Church for the arts and crafts. With all these notions they had
acquainted large numbers of Englishmen besides those few who
actually joined their sect. On the other hand, Lollardy had not

significantly developed and popularized that Pauline-Augustinian doctrine which became the key to Luther's system: justification by faith alone.

While the links between Wycliffism and Bohemia had long since perished, those between the Hussites and the Waldensians had become closer, especially after the visit by Luke of Prague to Florence in 1498. Various of Luke's writings were translated into the dialect of the Cottian Alps. Even on the popular level, the connection occasionally comes to light. A group of six naïve Waldensians, questioned in Paesana in 1510, declared their hope in the coming of a great Messiah-King from Bohemia, who would destroy and expropriate the churches, slay the clerics, abolish inequitable taxation in favour of a simple poll-tax, and introduce property-communism. The Florentine congregation known to Luke still evidenced a capacity displayed centuries earlier by the followers of Peter Waldo: the capacity to discover and then to absorb local heterodox groups in distant places. While the chief strength of Waldensianism lay in the Alpine valleys, it could boast a training school in Milan and offshoots as far away as Calabria and Apulia. Having an independent novitiate and ordination-service, the Waldensians despatched into the field a considerable force of itinerant missionaries, who, much like their Lollard equivalents, committed to memory long passages from the Gospels and Epistles. In general these cautious sectarians attended Catholic services in addition to their own. They believed in a simplified Gospel-Christianity which rejected purgatory and saint-worship, and they usually upheld a symbolic interpretation of the eucharist foreshadowing that of Zwingli. They disliked making confession, especially to unworthy priests. They were exposed at an early date to Protestant influence, for Guillaume Farel—in later years Calvin's famous associate—was at work among them by 1523. Under these new pressures some leaned to Zwinglianism and some to Lutheranism. Others tried to maintain the older Bohemian connection, while a great many long resisted Protestant attitudes on justification and predestination. The winning of the majority to Zwinglianism is generally held to date from a famous meeting held in September

1532 at Cianforan in the Angrogna Valley. Few of these people appear to have moved on into Anabaptism and through centuries of persecution they have maintained their identity to the present day. Like the Lollards, they could scarcely have made important conquests unaided by the new Protestantism; they too lacked intellectual and technical equipment; they offered little appeal to princes, to cities, to the propertied and political classes in general.

It would seem unrealistic to limit our review of heresy to these three organized churches, since there also existed other heterodox cells and tendencies which exercised marginal influences upon the Reformation. The radical wings of the latter, particularly its Anabaptist and Spiritualist groups, drew a measure of inspiration from old but heterodox currents of thought which persisted, though with few institutional traces, into the sixteenth century. One of these currents derived from the Calabrian prophet Abbot Joachim of Fiore, who died about 1202 and whose works had been widely popularized under the title *The Everlasting Gospel* by the Spiritual Franciscans of the thirteenth century. To Joachim's more thoroughgoing disciples, the sacraments were mere symbols destined to be superseded in the coming Age of the Holy Spirit, when love should rule the earth and the Scriptures be interpreted in a wholly new light. A far more orthodox school, yet one which also attracted a certain amount of suspicion, was that of the fourteenth-century contemplatives and of their successors of the pietist movement known as the *devotio moderna*, whose best-known monument is the *Imitation of Christ* attributed to Thomas à Kempis. The teaching of these mystics was less marked by pantheism than their critics alleged, yet it did in effect point toward an interior and non-institutional Christianity. These influences descended not merely upon Carlstadt, Müntzer and the 'Spiritualists', but upon Luther himself. In sharp contrast there also persisted many Catharist and antinomian ideas, floating loosely and not always integrated into coherent systems or held by organized bodies. In central Germany, in the Netherlands and elsewhere, little groups known as Brethren of the Free Spirit had since the thirteenth century combined pantheism and antinomianism with eschatological ideas resembling

7 The Ship of the Church navigates the shallows of heresy: wood-cut of 1528. Having passed the Scylla and Charybdis of Pelagianism and Predestination, the vessel is menaced by rocks of heresy ancient and modern: Huss and Wycliffe, Arius, the Waldensians, Mahomet. Chains attached to the stern are held by the World, the Flesh and the Devil

those of Joachim of Fiore. Some of these groups regarded unconventional patterns of sexual behaviour as marks of the perfected initiate. The erotic symbolism of Hieronymus Bosch (d. 1516) in his *The Garden of Delights* is linked by some scholars with the lore of the Brethren. Even in the mid-sixteenth century heretics holding similar complexes of belief were still being prosecuted near Nuremberg, near Mühlhausen and in Switzerland. Such local traditions of dissent could prove extremely tenacious and long-lived. Yet while it remains impossible accurately to assess the total influence of hole-and-corner heresies upon the Reformation sects, there appears no indication that they exerted decisive effects over large areas.

18

8 Hieronymus Bosch, *The Garden of Delights* (detail) ▶

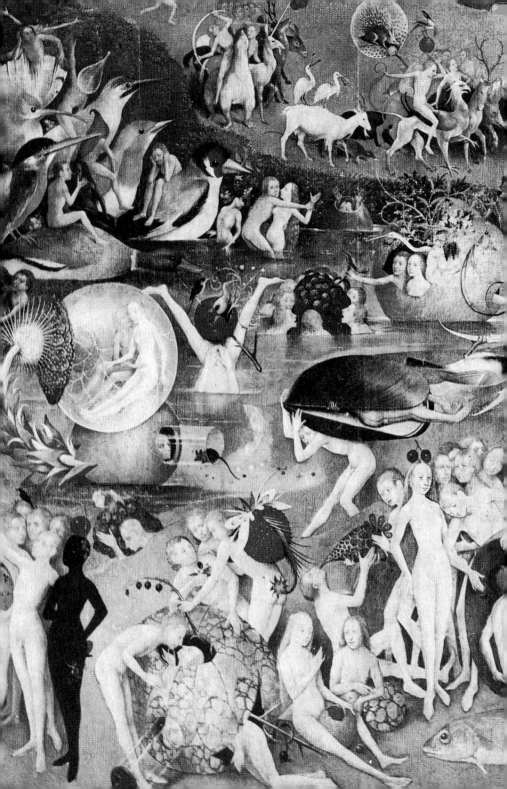

9 The philosopher: William of Occam's scepticism aided the disintegration of scholasticism: from a contemporary manuscript

10 The prelate: Stephen Gardiner, advocate under Henry VIII of a national but otherwise Catholic Church: anonymous painted portrait

11 The servant of the State: Thomas Cromwell, manager of the Henrician Reformation: portrait after Holbein the Younger

ANTIPAPALISM AND ERASTIANISM

While medieval dissent tended to lack intellectual appeal, the more intellectual critics of the Church had seldom held much attraction for her devouter sons. Erastianism, anticlericalism and antipapalism were nevertheless bound to flourish in a society which endowed churchmen with excessive power and wealth. An erastian tradition with some almost modern overtones originated with Dubois and other French nationalists who witnessed the clash between Philip IV and Boniface VIII. It grew to maturity a few decades later in a parallel context: that of the struggle between Emperor Louis of Bavaria and the French-controlled Papacy. The notorious *Defensor Pacis* (1324) by the Emperor's champion Marsiglio of Padua lived on not merely as a forerunner but as an active participant in the victories of sixteenth-century rulers over the Church. In England, for example, a printed translation of the *Defensor Pacis* was personally financed by the executive of the political Reformation, Thomas Cromwell. Meanwhile Cromwell's enemy Stephen Gardiner, though otherwise a stubborn Catholic, did not hesitate to reproduce Marsiglio's arguments in favour of a national church wholly divorced from the pope. Practical politicians like Cromwell and Gardiner found in the Paduan a rich fund of ideas. To him the State is the unifying principle in society and derives its authority from the whole people. The

Church holds property and jurisdiction solely by kind consent of the State. The episcopal hierarchy is of human and not divine institution, while the primacy of Rome arises merely from the Donation of Constantine, a document still accepted as genuine in Marsiglio's day. The priesthood should be concerned with the care of souls, not with judging men. In spiritual matters a General Council, including both priests and laymen, should hold ultimate authority.

Among the associates of Marsiglio in the service of the Emperor Louis had stood that eminent philosopher William of Occam, who likewise demanded the exclusion of the Church from temporal affairs, a larger share in Church life for the laity and sharp curbs on papal jurisdiction in favour of a system of national churches. Another Erastian only less radical than Marsiglio was John Wycliffe (*c.* 1329–84), who insisted that rightful lordship depended on Grace, demanded the disendowment of the Church by the State and at last banished papal authority to the realm of Antichrist. Before the middle of the fifteenth century a new phase of the assault developed when Lorenzo Valla (*c.* 1406–57) and Nicholas of Cusa (*c.* 1400–64), both papal officials, unmasked as forgeries two of the leading documents hitherto adduced in favour of the papal supremacy: the Donation of Constantine and the Isidorean Decretals.

The antipapal and erastian tradition inherited by the sixteenth century did not lie in the realm of theory alone. Especially in France, with its Pragmatic Sanction of Bourges (1438), and in England, with its Statutes of Provisors and Praemunire (1351–93), large powers over the national churches were conveyed from the Papacy to the monarchies. When in 1516 Leo X and Francis I agreed on the Concordat of Bologna, Gallican independence lay more firmly than ever in the grasp of the French crown, which could now nominate clerics to some 620 important preferments in cathedral churches and monasteries. Yet the control of Louis XII or of Francis I over ecclesiastical appointments and taxation need scarcely have been envied by Henry VII or by the young Henry VIII. These English kings suffered very little money to leave their realm for Rome. No pope interfered with their nominations to bishoprics, which in almost every case went to men who had earned favour in the royal service. Similarly the Catholic Kings became the effective masters of the Spanish Church, and here the reforms made by their great minister Cardinal Ximenes (d. 1517) kept at bay those abuses which elsewhere supplied ammunition to heretics and anticlericals. In all three countries a strong royal officialdom compounded of clerics and laymen developed an *esprit de corps* able to match that of any religious order, even that of the papal court itself. Under the strong western monarchies men had become sensible of their debt to princes, and the spirit of patriotism flowed through Church and State alike. In England, with its unique institutions of the common law and the Inns of Court, the whole legal fraternity was striving to erode clerical power long before the name of Luther resounded throughout Europe.

From this trend toward nationalized churches, Italy and Germany stood largely apart, since they lacked effective national monarchies. Some German princes had indeed acquired powers of visitation over their local churches and monasteries. Yet the Concordat of Vienna between Emperor Frederick III and Pope Nicholas V (1448) had furnished no such general safeguards as those protecting France or England, and with monotonous regularity each Diet presented *gravamina* against clerical extortions. The alarming language

12 Leo X (Giovanni de' Medici, Lorenzo's second son: Pope 1513–21): portrait-sketch attributed variously to Sebastiano del Piombo and Giulio Romano

employed by these official documents not only anticipated but rivalled that of Luther at his most abusive. In 1518 the Diet of Augsburg was confronted with the request of Leo X, made through Cardinal Cajetan, for a special tax to promote a crusade. It retorted that the real foe of Christendom was not the Turk but the 'hell-hound' in Rome. We can feel no surprise that the decisive revolt came from the Germans, who combined the most luxuriant religiosity with the most bitter anticlericalism. Under the influence of humanists like Celtis, Trithemius and Wimpfeling, a strong sentiment of German nationalism manifested itself in a species of antiquarian and cultural self-righteousness. It found itself confronting a blank wall of frustration, since Germany had failed to develop a political organization answering to this sense of national destiny or able to protect Germans against the fiscal and legal claims of Rome. Even without Luther's leadership, this frustration was bound to vent itself upon the Papacy. Again, it seems natural enough that the revolt —like that of the Hussites long before—should have arisen from a quasi-colonial frontier of Europe, where men felt themselves exploited in favour of the princes and communities of the anciently settled Mediterranean Basin and Rhine Valley.

23

13 The Pope gives his benediction from the balcony of the Vatican in old St Peter's Square: engraving by Claude Duchet, from his nephew Antoine Lafréry's *Speculum Romanae Magnificentiae* (Rome, 1575–83). Michelangelo's death in 1564 left the dome of the new basilica finished only as far as the drum

In Italy a different outlook prevailed. Here the sense of nationality stood ranged not against Rome, but against the 'barbarian' foreign powers which from 1494 to 1529 brought such misery and humiliation to Italians. The popes, enveloped in the serpent-coils of secular politics, inevitably attracted hatreds, but the Papacy remained a unique and ancient institution upon Italian soil: it continued to exercise world-wide functions in which even its Italian enemies might feel a sneaking pride. Full of scorn for ecclesiastical principalities and for the public credulity which exalted them, Machiavelli regarded the Papal States as the great barrier to Italian unification. Yet even he felt for Cesare Borgia a romantic admiration which outran the rather squalid facts, and he displayed an undisguised admiration for that great intriguer, warrior and state-builder Julius II, who entered with such skill into the heritage of the Borgias.

24

The most consistently anticlerical force in Italy, the most secular-minded society, the only Italian power ostensibly in a position to repress the Papacy, was Venice. Yet during the early years of the sixteenth century Venice stood in no position to lead Italians into an effective antipapal league, much less to force reforms upon the Church. By persistently grasping at an ever wider land-empire, she had terrified her neighbours and driven them into the arms of Julius II. In 1508–9 the resultant League of Cambrai came near to destroying Venice, but thenceforward the remorseless advance of Spanish power throughout Italy restricted the range of both papal and Venetian diplomacy. Again, the internal politics of the various Italian states did not favour the rise of reformers and prophets in opposition to Rome. These were places for serpents, not for doves. Without playing a violent or dramatic rôle, Alexander VI had not long to wait before Savonarola both offended Italian national sentiment and fell foul of the shifting Signoria of Florence. The latter then obliged Alexander by destroying the troublesome revivalist. Italian prophets had many local obstacles to surmount before they could become national figures and their best hope lay in obtaining papal patronage. Neither the State-system nor the amoral individualism nor the aestheticism of High Renaissance Italy left much scope for crusades to reform the Church. A genuine religious revival had already begun among the religious orders in Italy, but it represented no more than the earliest glimmer of a dawn slow to break. Meanwhile the great Italians could still show a cold and cynical ferocity

14 The Eagle and the Frog: an allusion, from Ulrich von Hutten's exhortation *To Emperor Maximilian* (1519), to the Habsburg quarrel with Venice. Wood-cut by Hans Weiditz

towards pope and clergy, a disdain more brutal than the complaints of any earnest barbarian north of the Alps. That great historian and papal official Francesco Guicciardini frankly averred that only self-interest prompted him to desire the aggrandisement of the popes. 'But for that', he adds, 'I should have loved Martin Luther as myself, not that I might throw off the laws laid down in the Christian religion as it is commonly interpreted and understood, but in order to see this gang of scoundrels brought within due bounds: that is, either rid of their vices or stripped of their authority.'

It would nevertheless be absurd to suppose that ordinary Europeans, even ordinary Italians, developed this mental dichotomy. In every country there were ambassadors and officials who had seen at first hand the luxury and pride of the Roman court. Yet most of these men themselves formed part of the clerical establishment and they had little incentive to return home and publicize the situation among their compatriots. In Germany the common man had a readier regard to the fiscal than to the moral liabilities of the Roman connection. The diaries of small Roman citizens—the sightless ants who crawled among the rising monuments of the Renaissance—suggest that even they knew little concerning the sins of the Borgias and the power-politics of Julius II. With all the more likelihood we may suppose that in 1510, even as Luther marvelled at the sights of Rome, ordinary Normans or Pomeranians or East Anglians were not yet deeply disturbed by the rumours of current Roman scandals. Yet Erasmus had already written his *Praise of Folly* and increasingly the arts of a corrosive journalism would be directed against the shortcomings of the clergy, both high and low.

18 The chief monument of the Renaissance in Rome, St Peter's basilica: late sixteenth-century engraving, with the other six great pilgrim churches of the city

II FURTHER CAUSES OF INSTABILITY

Even the briefest account of the intellectual forces which underlay the Reformation could not ignore the decline of philosophical theology and its replacement by a new type of biblical theology based on humanist scholarship. The brilliant attempt of St Thomas Aquinas to fuse Aristotelian philosophy with revealed Christianity had failed to win acceptance as the synthesis to end all syntheses. Even within the *Via Antiqua*—the Realist school descending from St Thomas—there had arisen renegades like Wycliffe, who found reasons to reject the steps which led to the crucial doctrine of transubstantiation. Meanwhile the *Via Moderna* or Nominalist school, headed by William of Occam, disputed the whole claim of philosophy to confirm or deny the data of revealed religion. Sharply separating reason from faith, Occam removed from the scope of the former the attributes, even the existence of God, together with the great dogmas of the Trinity and the Incarnation. His intellectual scepticism even extended to the position that a statement might be true in philosophy but false in theology. And however cautiously we need to review Luther's place in the *Via Moderna* tradition, the facts remain that he was educated by Occamists, that he exalted the primacy of faith and that he rejoiced in the overthrow of Thomist-Aristotelian Christianity.

By this time the whole scholastic approach had fallen into confusion and aridity. While it still provided a basic discipline in mental gymnastics, earnest men of religion were ceasing to believe that the world of scholastic reasoning offered a major road to divine truth. While Occam's anti-scholasticism was devastating this world from within, the mystics and pietists were dismissing all intellectualism as a broken reed. Meanwhile since the early decades of the fourteenth century the humanists had been at work in the Italian cities, laying

19 Jacques Lefèvre d'Étaples:
contemporary engraving

20 John Colet:
sketch by Holbein the Younger

the foundations of a literary, linguistic and historical discipline which likewise found scholasticism irrelevant. Without descending to argument, Petrarch had gently turned aside whenever he heard the brawling of logicians and philosophers. He and his followers transformed both the ideal of education and the art of living; they ended by giving a sense of superiority to those many aristocrats, city patricians and jurists who comprised the new educated classes and in this humanist sphere met clerics upon at least equal terms.

Headed by Erasmus, the Christian humanists of the earlier sixteenth century tended to regard Christ as an exemplar, a classical hero, a way of living rather than as the Saviour on the Cross. They saw in the Christian life the struggle of an essentially free and dignified being to control his selfhood and his appetites. If thus they stood directly opposed to Protestantism, they also despised monkery and the trivial cults of popular religion. They could not form churches or attract the masses; differing among themselves on so many issues, they would seem to represent a cultural trend, not a school of thought, still less a Reformation in its own right.

Christian humanism was loose, many-coloured, pervasive among both Protestants and Catholics, less of a third force than a dilution of the other two. It could nevertheless boast some positive religious concomitants, the most important of which lay in the extension of its historical and philological techniques to the Greek and Hebrew texts of the Bible. As early as 1496–7 John Colet returned to England

30

from Italy, where he had learned Greek, and delivered those famous Oxford lectures on the Pauline Epistles which so clearly demonstrate the new approach. He strove to see the Apostle Paul as a real man in a real setting, to understand the New Testament by close reference to its historical background, to concentrate upon the literal sense of the Epistles as if they had been a text of Quintillian or Cicero. Heading a reform-party in the English Church, Colet ended by encountering accusations of heresy. So did Johannes Reuchlin (1455–1522), whose *De Rudimentis Hebraicis* (1506) enabled Christian scholars to begin studying the Old Testament upon the necessary bases of Jewish scholarship. So did the evangelical humanist Jacques Lefèvre (*c.* 1455–1536), librarian of the monastery of St Germain des Prés, who in 1512 published an edition of the Pauline Epistles with a commentary anticipating some of the emphases of Luther. Unlike the latter, Lefèvre respected the institutions of the Church and merely called for their reform. On the other hand, he pronounced the New Testament to be 'the book of life and the sole rule of Christians'; he declared divine grace the only source of salvation,

21, 22 (*Below*) The savaging of this portrait of Erasmus from the Basle, 1550, edition of Sebastian Münster's *Cosmographia*, is the work of the Spanish Inquisition: Münster's own is among other portraits thus defaced. (*Right*) Erasmus painted by Holbein the Younger, 1523

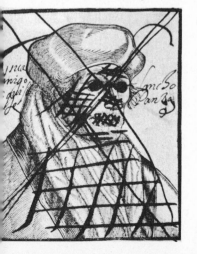

good works being merely the outward sign of a justifying faith. He doubted the sacrificial character of the Mass and stressed the aspect of a memorial-service. He denied that monasticism was a superior way of life and said that penance lost its salutary character if it induced men to trust in their own works of satisfaction instead of those wrought for them by Christ. In 1516 his abbot Guillaume Briçonnet was translated to the bishopric of Meaux: four years later, worried by the savage attacks of the Sorbonne, Lefèvre and his followers went thither and participated in the efforts of Briçonnet to reform the diocese.

Between Colet, Reuchlin, Lefèvre and Erasmus many distinctions may be made, yet the unifying feature of this great phase of humanism cannot be missed: it lies in a historical approach to the 'prescribed texts' of the Christian religion. These men were seriously trying to penetrate the clouds of ecclesiastical accretion and of irresponsible fantasy; they were attempting to answer the question: what exactly did Christ and St Paul teach? And how should their teachings be understood in the context of that distant age of primitive Christianity?

In view of the official rigidities of our period this approach was always potentially disruptive, yet it was not wholly new. Two centuries before Reuchlin the great biblical scholar of Paris, Nicholas of Lyra, had possessed a knowledge of Hebrew and of some Jewish expositors. He had insisted upon the unremitting duty of scholars to seek the precise and literal sense of the Bible, as opposed to the imaginative allegorizing of the schoolmen. His works frequently appear in the inventories of sixteenth-century clergymen and he was blamed by some conservatives as an inspirer of Luther. Nearer still to our period, Lorenzo Valla had written those *Annotations on the New Testament* which in 1505 Erasmus saw fit to publish. By taking three Latin and three Greek manuscripts, Valla had shown that they often differed from each other, that in some cases the Latin was a mistranslation of the Greek, and that mistranslation could vitally affect matters of faith and Church government.

Along these prophetic lines the generation of Reuchlin and Erasmus, aided by a fuller linguistic apparatus, established the ideas that the Vulgate text had not been handed down from Sinai with a divine *imprimatur*. Men must go behind it to seek the meaning of the original Hebrew and Greek words; it was permissible to argue over the primitive meanings of words like *presbyteros, episkopos* and *ekklesia*, and to ask whether *metanoeite* should not be translated 'repent' rather than (as in the Vulgate) 'do penance'. These matters were far from being purely academic in their implications. Considering also that he accompanied such findings with a stream of satire against ecclesiastical corruption, Erasmus bore a charmed life, protected by high fashion, petted and flattered by a host of eminent churchmen. Humanists or would-be humanists, these prelates in their public capacity as judges could still with good consciences burn plebeian heretics for making a demand substantially similar to that of Erasmus: the demand for a Christianity based closely upon the New Testament. Even in Spain the influence of Erasmus remained strong for several decades, although in 1537 the Inquisition prohibited the reading of his books in Spanish and ordered even the Latin editions to be expurgated. By this time their author was dead, and it was not until 1559 that the Roman Index imposed a general ban on his writings. During the time Erasmus and those more amusing satirists of the *Epistolae Obscurorum Virorum* (1515, 1517) were at work, persecution was poorly co-ordinated and seldom directed against men of eminence. If one avoided political intrigue and the more delicate issues of sacramental dogma, many things damaging to ecclesiastical prestige and custom might still be written with impunity. Jacques Lefèvre was condemned in 1521 by the Sorbonne, but even when driven from Meaux he never lacked powerful protectors and he died aged eighty-two at Nérac, the court of Marguérite of Angoulême, sister of Francis I. Against the persecutors of Reuchlin there arose a counterblast of ridicule which did much to create the atmosphere of Luther's Germany. And while the reactionary Dominicans of Cologne, the inquisitor Jakob Hochstraten and the renegade humanist Ortuin Gratius were smallish game, bigger targets could sometimes be sighted. In *Julius Exclusus*, commonly attributed to Erasmus, the author dared to show St Peter driving the warlike pontiff himself from the gates of paradise.

The reality of many abuses attacked by these humanists was admitted by the intelligent Catholics of the younger generation. Many of them were attacked afresh by Cardinals Contarini, Caraffa, Pole and Sadoleto in the *Consilium de Emendanda Ecclesia* presented to the Pope in 1537. Even this document does not hesitate to lay much of the blame on the popes themselves, and it was presently re-published in German by Luther, along with his own gleeful comments. Such sources inevitably suggest a further comparison of causes. How far in fact were Protestant and radical movements provoked or furthered by the indiscretions of worldly ecclesiastics? How far did they arise from the inadequacies of late medieval religion, or from the blind traditionalism of theological faculties? How far, again, from the educational, economic and technical changes now besetting society? Such comparisons lend themselves to academic exercises rather than to confident answers, yet the evidence for all these causes of instability remains massive enough. To a certain point, this evidence can be defined and analysed.

CHURCH ABUSES AND PUBLIC OPINION

The popular image of a shrewd, clever, intriguing Papacy may owe more to the famous portraits of popes and their *nipoti* by Raphael and Titian than to the hard facts of history. After all, the Renaissance pontiffs committed some of the greatest blunders in the long history of the Holy See. Triumphant over the Councils, Rome rebuilt that spiritual absolutism which was to culminate in the Counter Reformation. It also continued to narrow and to Italianize itself in a multitude of senses. Increasingly it used funds intended for the central needs of the Church as a means to aggrandize itself among the other Italian powers. The creation of an effective State across central Italy, the building of a monumental metropolis, the enlargement of the college of cardinals to give a great majority of compliant Italians, the underestimation of naïve moralism north of the Alps, the absorption in the fairylands of art-patronage and pygmy-politics; above all, the pursuit of Medici family-interests by Leo X and Clement VII: all these preoccupations and misunderstandings had greatly lowered the horizons of the popes. They had become less

23 Luther's service (left) is attended by the sacrificial Christ and the Elector John Frederick, while the Pope (right) hawks indulgences. The bull he flourishes bears a variant of Johann Tetzel's jingle (cf. ill. 46). The violent dualism must have had an irresistible popular appeal

European than when they lay at Avignon under the tutelage of France. Their local ambitions involved them in an insensitive fiscalism all the more perilous since the stronger rulers of Europe had diverted it to less united and stable countries like Germany. Moreover, the ethical and theological bases of this fund-raising were becoming dubious by any standards. In 1476 Sixtus IV had extended the scope of an Indulgence even to souls in purgatory, thus exploiting for cash the natural anxieties of simple people for their departed relatives. Luther's initial revolt was provoked by this spectacle of a salvation assurance company with branches in heaven, earth and purgatory.

Some almost equally incautious expedients appear in the field of secular Roman finance. Leo X realized about half-a-million ducats annually from the sale of some 2,000 offices, mostly sinecures which men purchased like annuities for a down-payment of about ten times the annual income of the post. Likewise in the fields of diplomacy and propaganda the Renaissance popes exemplified Italy's

35

over-cleverness, its excessive confidence in its peninsular values, in its ability to handle the foreign barbarian by superior adroitness. They tolerated, even exemplified, that peculiar blend of corruption, individualism and sophistication which set Italy apart from the rest of Europe and so invited Machiavelli's heroic call for a purifying dictatorship. All this and more may be said against the Renaissance Papacy, provided we remember some enormous counterbalancing facts: that the popes were Italian princes willy-nilly, that they had to struggle for a precarious independence, that other rulers (especially the pious Habsburgs) shamelessly strove to manipulate papal powers without making nice distinctions between sacred and secular policies. The Renaissance popes were as much sinned against as sinning.

While Rome lost its antennae and became remote from the nations of Europe, the prelates of the Church had long tended to lose contact with their clergy and people. Diocesan bishops had centuries ago become feudal lords. The episcopates of Europe were compounded partly of aristocrats, partly of officials rewarded for their labours in the service of princes and commonly continuing those secular labours after their elevation to bishoprics. Apart from high birth, a doctorate in the civil law, followed by a few ambassadorial missions or a few years in a chancery, was a far surer road to high preferment than sanctity of character, eminence in sacred learning, missionary activities or even ecclesiastical administration. Ascetics and reformers like Ximenes or John Fisher were as yet exceptional figures in the upper reaches of the Church. The best-intentioned prelates could hardly modify a system sanctioned by popes and princes, a system from which they themselves had sprung. And the notion that a bishop's work should be done in his absence by suffragans, chancellors, registrars and other subordinates had ample parallels lower down in the Church. At every level it was accepted that office-holders should draw their stipends and hire working deputies at much lower rates. In the parishes absentee incumbents collected tithes but appointed ill-paid chaplains to serve the cures; in cathedrals canons enjoyed lucrative prebends while humble vicars choral conducted the services.

So far as the people were concerned, ecclesiastical authority tended not only to seem impersonal, but to present itself in legal rather than in pastoral guise. Canon law, an international code locally modified by national and provincial decrees, may have seemed to 'advanced' critics a mere ghost of imperial Rome, yet it still held all Christian men in its firm grip. It was administered by the Roman Curia and by a descending hierarchy of ecclesiastical courts throughout Europe. It held jurisdiction in many spheres—testaments, slander, matrimony, sexual offences—which have in more recent times been absorbed by state law. In the church courts most crimes could be compounded by paying fines. 'The Lord desireth not the death of a sinner', conceded a papal official, 'but rather that he should pay and live'. A most profitable source of income arose from the grant of dispensations, especially those allowing marriages within the prohibited degrees. This trade had been enormously multiplied by imaginative theologians, who established spiritual relationships even between unrelated people if they merely became god-parents to the same infant. The tariff, however carefully graded, was heavy. In the succinct words of another frank papal official: 'note carefully, that

24, 25 Christ ascends; the Pope plunges, attended by devils and familiars, into Hell: the last of a series of such contrasts published by Cranach the Elder in 1521

such privileges and dispensations are not conceded to poor people'. In so far as the partial collapse of Catholicism can be blamed on its own shortcomings, it may primarily be blamed on the habit of seeing organized religion in terms of law and finance rather than in terms of spiritual education. While the vision of God the Judge terrified sensitive consciences like that of the young Luther, the spectacle of the Church as judge inspired an open enmity in more worldly men. And if the ultimate recovery of Catholicism may chiefly be ascribed to any one process, it should so be ascribed to a correction of this fatal unbalance.

The stratification of the Church did not in itself shock a feudal society which accepted both celestial and terrestrial hierarchies as decreed by divine providence. Few Frenchmen can have been scandalized even when Cardinal John of Lorraine was appointed coadjutor of Metz at the tender age of three, or when his nephew Charles of Guise received the archbishopric of Rheims at fourteen, and later became bishop of Metz, administrator of the bishopric of Verdun, abbot of ten abbeys and Cardinal of Lorraine. Many of the German bishoprics and abbacies likewise became the properties of great families. The indulgences castigated by Luther arose from the financial needs of that sybaritic prelate Albert of Brandenburg, who at the age of twenty-four was not content to travel about with his mistresses piquantly if tactfully clad in male costume. Already Archbishop of Magdeburg and administrator of Halberstadt, he wished to accede to the archbishopric of Mainz, and agreed to pay Leo X 21,000 ducats as entry-fee, together with 10,000 ducats for confirmation in all his offices. Through princely favour, men of less exalted ancestry might sometimes amass a comparable group of benefices. Cardinal d'Estouteville had in France one archbishopric, three bishoprics, four abbeys and three priories, but they did not prevent him from spending most of his time in Italy, where he held a further bishopric. Thomas Wolsey's preferments would take as long to list, while Thomas Winter, his illegitimate and quite undistinguished schoolboy son, held a great number of prebends and other benefices yielding about 250 times the income of an English country parson.

Pluralism and absenteeism were not regarded with modern eyes. That denouncer of clerical sloth and avarice John Colet was himself a pluralist, while conversely the arch-pluralist Charles of Guise became a reforming prelate. While there are some recorded exceptions, most men doubtless accepted what would now be considered gross nepotism, systematic income-building and even simony. The unpopularity of Thomas Wolsey arose less from the grand total of his income than from other exceptional factors: that he combined his ecclesiastical offices with the Lord Chancellorship of England; that his Chancery jurisdiction competed with that of the common law courts; that he invaded the jurisdictions of other clerics or drew heavy blackmail for leaving them unmolested; that by purchasing wardships he oppressed noble and gentle families. Above all he was a social upstart, excessively addicted to arrogant display. Yet there were certainly some few intelligent laymen who resented the ease with which lucky clerics amassed large revenues. The industrious lawyer and merchant Thomas Cromwell became Wolsey's business-manager, but he did not hesitate to taunt the cardinal's over-rewarded chaplains for their avarice as they all sat together at dinner.

26, 27, 28 Monkish covetousness was unmasked for critical contemporaries by this grim toy: sinister from the first, the monk becomes, as the flaps are lifted, a ravening wolf and an ingurgitator of property. The supplicating widow and her child seem from another world

At the other end of the scale a parish priest in a poor living or the incumbent of a chantry might receive little more than the wage of an unskilled labourer. The former could count himself fortunate if he still had a glebe to plough on weekdays. His tasks were hardly conducive to study or self-improvement; his Latin usually extended to the correct celebration of mass, but far less often to reading Augustine or Erasmus. Everywhere in Europe angry voices were raised against clerical ignorance and against the superfluous ordinations of candidates ill-qualified by learning. Needless to add, many of these mundane priests failed to observe the law of celibacy. Concubinage had become flagrant in many parts of Europe and had at least brought less disrepute upon the Church than promiscuity. Lay malice and hypocrisy made the most of the facts and it requires little knowledge of sixteenth-century anticlerical propaganda to realize how heavily the Church paid for debarring marriage to its secular clergy.

This ordination of priests without proper financial support was encouraged by the belief that the mere multiplication of Masses could shorten the torments of a soul in purgatory. The rich, who could buy Masses on a grand scale, left nothing to chance. On the other hand, poorer men eagerly wanted to believe Luther when he denounced such investment as meaningless, and amid a general spirit of revulsion many people proceeded to wider rejections of Catholic sacramental doctrine. This was the bitter fruit of a belief soon to be denounced as erroneous by reformed Catholicism itself.

Concerning the regular clergy, brief judgements are apt to be inaccurate, for monasticism had produced luxuriant variety, the more luxuriant if we include the heavily populated orders of friars, and those of regular canons who often served cures outside the cloister. Certain houses, particularly those of the *élite* Carthusian Order, continued to produce saints and to enjoy a shining reputation. The Observant movement to tighten discipline among the friars dated from the fourteenth century; it was promoted in Spain by that great Franciscan Ximenes and culminated in 1529 with the founding of the Capuchins. It thus merged with the new wave of religious orders which formed an early phase of the Catholic Reformation.

Even as Luther brandished the torch of revolt, in Italy the capacity of the Church for self-improvement was being modestly yet not unimpressively demonstrated by the reform and expansion of the Camaldolese (1520), the founding of the Theatins (confirmed in 1524) and the early meetings of the Oratory of Divine Love (from 1517). In both old and new universities monks and friars continued active and numerous, both as teachers and as students. The property-less friars had a low stake in the establishment and tended to sym-pathize with radical and popular causes. Many of them were to throw off their cowls and figure prominently as Protestant Reformers. Yet while the world of the regulars was far from wholly static on the eve of the Reformation, it cannot be denied that the older religious orders had become listless and custom-ridden; their flame no longer burned brightly or reflected much light into the outer world.

POPULAR CULTS AND THE NEW DEVOTION

While the shortcomings of the clergy promoted anticlericalism, they did not necessarily predispose people to accept the positive doctrines of Luther and Zwingli. If we search for the predisposing factors, we are more likely to find some of them in the religious idioms of the later Middle Ages. Though it would be misleading to claim that two Catholic religions coexisted around 1500, it may be said that ortho-doxy was a Janus with two very different faces: one popular, the other more esoteric. The first was the cult of saints, pilgrimages and relics, the world of the *Golden Legend*. Never in the social history of the Christian faith had the saints been so demanding, and while this near-polytheism softened many a rough and aggressive mind, it was apt to seem a very remote derivative of Christianity when people began to read the New Testament for themselves. These cults were by no means limited to the simple, and the refined ridicule of Erasmus cannot be accepted as a typical upper-class attitude. By 1518 Luther's strange protector Frederick the Wise of Saxony had gathered in his collegiate church of All Saints Wittenberg a lucrative hoard of 17,000 relics, including a piece of Moses' burning bush, parts of the holy cradle and swaddling clothes, thirty-three fragments of the holy cross and no less than 204 assorted portions of the Holy

Innocents. About the same time the young Henry VIII made the pilgrimage to Walsingham in bare feet, while it was there also that Erasmus offered to Our Lady the unusually sophisticated tribute of a Greek ode.

The other face of late medieval Catholicism was the *devotio moderna*, its deeper stratum the great mystical literature of the fourteenth century—Eckhart, Tauler, Suso, Ruysbroeck, Rolle and Hilton—its later stratum the beneficent and far less cloistered quietism best illustrated by the Brethren of the Common Life. These laymen of the Netherlands and Lower Rhineland renounced private property and led regulated lives in community, yet without taking irrevocable vows. They laid stress on practical piety and character rather than upon ritualism or theological analysis. While not creative humanists, they accepted humanist pedagogy and their schools became justly famous. The one at Deventer could boast Thomas à Kempis and Nicholas of Cusa among its early pupils,

29, 30 Frederick the Wise, Elector of Saxony, 1496, by Dürer; and a wood-cut from a catalogue of the Elector's famous collection of relics, showing his silver monstrance containing thorns from the crown of Christ

31 Mathis Grünewald, *Crucifixion:* from the Isenheim Altarpiece
(completed 1515–16)

Erasmus among those of a later period. Throughout the literary
career of Erasmus the *devotio* was taking full advantage of the printing presses; its great classic the *Imitation of Christ* now spread its ideas
throughout Europe and had a message for every devoted soul, from
the Anabaptists to St Ignatius Loyola himself. During the great
conflicts of the sixteenth century mystical writings were also widely
utilized by the various contenders, especially by the radicals. Thomas
Müntzer had as his vade-mecum, bound together in one volume, the
sermons of Tauler and the collection of mystical and visionary
writings *Liber trium virorum et spiritualium virginum*, edited by
Lefèvre and published at Paris in 1513. Soon after the latter date
Luther himself was deeply affected not only by Tauler but by the
Theologia Germanica, a work written in the same tradition near the
end of the fourteenth century by a priest of the Teutonic Order of

43

Sachsenhausen. The more hectic phases of this heritage find illustration in the great *Isenheim Altarpiece* by Mathis Neithardt, called Grünewald, who painted this in 1512–15 and died in 1528. It comes as no surprise to discover strong indications that he was perilously involved in the radical and revolutionary movements of the 'twenties.

Profound and ubiquitous as the influence of the *devotio* became, it lacked the power to supply the new age with a stabilizing synthesis. Despite the optimism of their advocates, these techniques of contemplation were too difficult—except in their most elementary phases—for men and women living in a harsh and busy world. To a hard-thinking, contentious, outspoken generation the *devotio* proposed a private ardour, not a fight against abuses. To an age making great intellectual discoveries and on the threshold of even greater ones, it offered a resolute anti-intellectualism:

> 'For though thou didst know the whole Bible by heart and the sayings of the philosophers, what doth it profit thee without the love of God? . . . Surely a humble husbandman that serveth God is better than a proud philosopher who, neglecting himself, labours to understand the movements of the heavens.'

When Thomas à Kempis set this tone for the movement, he was certainly not foreseeing the age of Calvin and of Copernicus. By this time the *devotio moderna* was not nearly modern enough. The new age was symbolized not by the grave and contemplative Deventer of the last century but by the international business-world of Antwerp and Augsburg, or by Dürer's Nuremberg, with its European commerce and its attractive fusion of Italianate humanism and German technology. The dominant elements of the new Europe were the lawyers, merchants, bankers, industrialists, bureaucrats, ambassadors, publicists, printers, designers and skilled craftsmen, men of courts and cities with increasing educational attainments and broadening horizons. Neither face of the ecclesiastical Janus could they find satisfying. Too critical to be held by the popular cults, they had little use for a semi-monastic religion of withdrawal and contemplation. They welcomed a more clear-cut and combative attack on the problems of their age. Too often self-deceived by the rationalizing of greed, of power, of self-interest, they nevertheless thought and planned in terms of rational reforms, whether on a Protestant or on a Catholic basis.

THE SECULAR FORCES

The political, social and economic forces working for or against the Reformation would defeat any attempt at a brief summary. Many will become apparent in the chapters which follow, but at the outset it may be profitable to enumerate a few which might otherwise escape due attention. We have already emphasized the internal efficiency and the advancing Erastianism of the more advanced monarchies of Europe. Without at first openly rejecting the supranational pretensions of the Church, these monarchies were demanding and receiving an ever more exclusive loyalty from their subjects: from bishops attuned to autocracy by studies in Roman law down to humble traders, who at least realized that the strong arm of royal officialdom protected their daily bread. While in Germany the claims of the princes had become almost as sweeping, the economic and cultural vitality of the innumerable towns and cities also fostered secular allegiances. Within these communities we must reckon not only with humanist oligarchs but with the growth of literacy even among the artisans, and with the continual transit of a floating population of traders, miners, preachers and mobile craftsmen. In Italy and the Netherlands the prevalence of town life and civic loyalties had long been striking. The influence of these urban values expanded far beyond their original points of impact. Even in Poland, increasingly drawn into the European orbit by the growth of her maritime and overland trade, the dominant social group of landowners was becoming deeply involved with that humanist intellectual life born in the cities and courts of western Europe. In France and still more impressively in England, great complexes of gentry, officials, lawyers, professional men, industrialists and merchants emerged from the status of clientage to the magnates. In alliance with the monarchies such middling and non-feudal elements gained political weight, acquired higher education and became susceptible to Erasmian and Protestant ideas. Particularly in England,

Rom
Maylan
Venedig
Infprucf
Offen
Nurmberg
Craca
Untorff
Lifbona

HER · IACOB · FVGGER

32 The new men of
Germany. Jacob Fugger
'the Rich', the Emperor's
banker, with his chief
accountant Matthäus
Schwarz: painted miniature
of 1519

33 The new European city. Nuremberg:
panorama in pen and watercolour,
about 1520, by Hans Wurm

their economic weight was soon to be enhanced by their purchases of lands taken from the Church.

Scarcely anywhere in Europe did the Reformation encounter a quiescent, a satisfied, an apathetic society. There were too many underdogs—and too many dissatisfied with the bones and scraps offered them in this world by any current social philosophies. In both town and countryside the element of class-struggle never lay far below the surface, though its character is not always elucidated by the vocabulary of nineteenth-century socialism. Landlords aided by their lawyers sought assiduously to extend their manorial rights and to circumscribe those of their tenants and serfs. The peasants, despised and distrusted in many parts of Europe as ill-tamed beasts of burden, responded by sporadic confederacies and riots. Likewise both the guilds and the unprivileged artisans strove to extract concessions from the ruling oligarchies of the towns. Again, as the century drew on, monetary inflation complicated all economic relationships, the more severely since its causes and nature were so little comprehended. That humble aristocrat of history, the potato, had not yet arrived to relieve the horror of bad harvests. The interactions between social-economic tensions and religious change inevitably demand examination. For pious and superstitious men, mundane and spiritual events interpenetrated each other. Pressures clearly economic in origin could readily be diverted by publicists and prophets towards religious and especially towards millenarian objectives. On the other hand, it has been urged with force that the

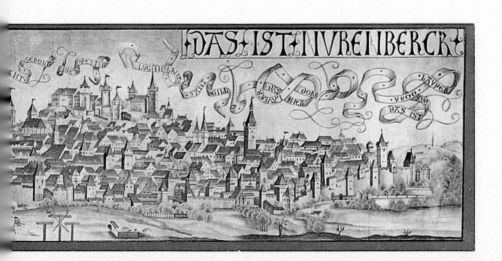

34 This 'Tree of Society', a wood-cut by Hans Weiditz, appeared in the Augsburg, 1532 edition in German of Petrarch's *De Remediis Utriusque Fortunae* (*c.* 1366), which would be known to Elizabethan readers as *Phisicke against Fortune, as well prosperous as adverse.* The cut is conventional until we reach the top, where the peasants reappear, one of them piping insouciantly. That this translation was largely the work of Spalatin reinforces the impression that the artist is referring to the unquiet social order

sixteenth century was not exceptionally marked by social and economic revolution, that it saw, for example, less radical changes than the seventeenth. In short, we can detect no simple pattern of causation, either intellectual, or economic, or even a combination of these two. Amid all nations and social groups there flourished a host of irrational forces: a preoccupation with diabolic agencies, witchcraft and sortilege, a curious blend of eschatological expectancy with a dread of universal dissolution. Disease, insecurity and the shortness of life not only urged men to thoughts of salvation but made them listen eagerly to apocalyptic teachings and yearn for sudden changes which would usher in an age of gold. To understand the bizarre imagination of the age, we should study the world of Hieronymus Bosch; if we seek a visual compendium of its human predicament, we may find one in Dürer's *The Four Horseman of the Apocalypse.*

48

35 The obsession of the age:
*The Four Horsemen of the
Apocalypse*, wood-cut by Dürer

Alongside all these broader changes, the half-century or more preceding Luther's revolt was marked by two particular developments which exerted great influence upon religious history: a spate of university foundations, and the rapid rise of book-production. The rôle of universities as centres of religious revolt could not be regarded as wholly novel when Luther made Wittenberg the spearhead of his movement. Wycliffe's movement had sprung from the clerks of Oxford, and there Jerome of Prague had studied it before returning about 1402 to his native university, where Huss was rector. The sensational outcome of these academic exchanges had not prevented orthodox rulers and prelates from undertaking a programme of university expansion. Between 1450 and 1517 no less than nine new universities came to birth in Germany alone, the last but one and the most modest being that of Wittenberg (1502). In France, Valence, Nantes and Bourges appeared between 1459 and

49

1464; in Spain some seven between 1450 and 1504. While England remained content with its two collegiate universities, many colleges were added to each of them. Cambridge overtook Oxford and was soon to become the cradle of English Lutheranism, later that of English Puritanism. Even the less wealthy countries set up their native establishments, Hungary at Pressburg (1465), Sweden at Uppsala (1477), Denmark at Copenhagen (1478). Scotland saw new colleges at St Andrews and new universities at Glasgow (1450) and Aberdeen (1494). The importance of both old and new academies in the ferment of ideas needs no demonstration. In later times it was to be acknowledged by the Jesuits, who put forth superhuman efforts to capture or recapture those universities and schools from which their battle for recovery could best be waged. Yet university opinion proved far from uncontrollable and far from invariably wedded to movements of reform or Reformation. The huge university of Paris had tended of late to lose its cosmopolitan character and to show itself increasingly erastian and patriotic. Yet its doctrinal conservatism during the age of the Reformation never seriously faltered; its collective prestige and the writings of its Catholic theologians exercised a most appreciable restraint upon religious change in France and throughout western Europe.

Both as an art and as an industry, printing had already attained a considerable degree of maturity before the advent of Lutheran

36 'The Bookseller': wood-cut by Hans Weiditz from Petrarch, *Trostspiegel* (*De Remediis*)

Protestantism. We know the names of a thousand printers operating *before* the year 1500, and the titles of about 30,000 books which they produced. With the new century there followed a still heavier output, including a large proportion of cheap books aimed at mass audiences. Between 1517 and 1520 Luther's thirty publications probably sold well over 300,000 copies. Despite the rise of secular interests throughout the century, religious books continued to enjoy immense sales as public literacy expanded. Altogether, in relation to the spread of religious ideas it seems difficult to exaggerate the significance of the Press, without which a revolution of this magnitude could scarcely have been consummated. Unlike the Wycliffite and Waldensian heresies, Lutheranism was from the first the child of the printed book, and through this vehicle Luther was able to make exact, standardized and ineradicable impressions upon the mind of Europe. For the first time in human history a great reading public judged the validity of revolutionary ideas through a mass-medium which used the vernacular languages together with the arts of the journalist and the cartoonist. Bishops and even kings had no police forces capable of sheltering their subjects from these wiles; their best recourse was to enter the business of book-production on their own account. And those who did so found in the ranks of the humanists a large force of *condottieri* ready to fight with apparent conviction for quite modest pay.

37, 38 'The divine art of printing': wood-cuts by Jost Amman from the *Book of Trades*, 1559

III LUTHER'S OUTLOOK AND IDEAS

To that perennial task, the examination of the young Luther, the help of the psychiatrist should be welcomed. Yet most historians feel unconvinced by recent attempts to 'explain' Luther's revolt as a belated effort to achieve independence against a masterful father and a severe mother. The selection of three or four sentences from the voluminous and rather unreliable *Table Talk* can scarcely replace the examination of a patient under clinical conditions. On the whole evidence, Luther's childhood seems strikingly 'normal' and his relations with his parents continued affectionate to the end of their long lives. Again, revolts and spiritual crises were matters of frequent experience, yet there was only one Luther. The psychiatrist cannot 'explain' that great machine of theology which tore Christendom asunder. When, on the other hand, we regard his educational and early intellectual influences, we stand indeed on firmer documentary ground, yet even these factors cannot explain the depth of Luther's personal experience and conviction, the richness and coherence of his personal synthesis, the dynamism with which he projected his message into the world of his time. In the last resort, Luther painfully hewed his own road through the hard rocks of the Bible. He is always so vastly bigger than those catalogues of influences with which we rationalizing historians of ideas inevitably preface our accounts.

At Erfurt and as an Augustinian friar he was trained in the Occamist *Via Moderna* by disciples of its last great teacher Gabriel Biel. From this school he doubtless absorbed some of his feeling for the majesty, the freedom, the omnipotence of God. To the Occamists God became intelligible not through man's favourite weapon of reason but through his own acts of self-revelation. Salvation depended solely upon acceptance by God, who in his omnipotence would accept even a sinner devoid of merits and good works. Yet

39 Luther preaching to his parishioners: detail from the predella of the altarpiece ▶
in the Town Church, Wittenberg, by Cranach the Elder

Eyn geyſtlich edles Buchleynn: von rechter vnderſcheyd vnd vorſtand, was der alt vñ new menſche ſey. Was Adams vñ was gottis kind ſey. vñ wie Ad. ynn vns ſterben vnnd Chriſtus erſteen ſall.

40 Luther's first published work: title-page of his edition of the *German Theology*, Wittenberg, 1516

41 Erfurt in about 1525: anonymous painting on wood. The Augustinian cloister is in the right foreground

in their eyes man remained a free agent, able to do something to make himself worthier of this acceptance. This last view Luther was to reject. His rigorous denial of free will and the efficacy of good works did not come from Occamism; neither did his mature teaching that men are justified by the imputation of Christ's righteousness to cover their sin. All in all, Occamist philosophy and theology did not so much provide Luther with key-doctrines as give him a training in the subtleties of scholastic discipline and a prejudice against that fusion of Aristotelian philosophy with Christianity which had been the great achievement of St Thomas Aquinas. On the other hand Luther did not apparently encounter Occam's antipapal writings during his training, while Gabriel Biel, his chief guide to Occamism, had reverted to an impeccable papalism.

It may also be said with certainty that the example of John Huss did not precipitate Luther into revolt. During his disputation with Eck in July 1519 Luther refused in decisive terms to be classed with the Bohemian heretics. By 1521 he had begun to refer to Huss as 'St John', but then his protest had already attained full stature, and we are bound to regard Hussitism as a confirmatory not a creative influence. Likewise a reading of Valla increased his anger against the Papacy, but this happened in 1520. Towards the mystics, Luther incurred far more vital obligations. In his Erfurt days he had read Dionysius, Bernard, Bonaventura and Gerson. His spiritual director Staupitz urged him to turn from scholastic theology to the sermons

54

of Johann Tauler, a copy of which he seems to have been constantly annotating from 1516. Here he found ample emphasis on the vanity of mere human attempts to please God, together with an obvious anticipation of his own insistence upon the passivity of the human will in its reception of the divine spirit. When in the same year he edited the *Theologia Germanica* with an enthusiastic introduction, he assumed it to be another work by Tauler. Two years later he republished it in a completer text. Luther shared the longing of the mystics for an interior religion based on the communion of the humble and receptive soul with God. Yet while to this extent he followed the *devotio* tradition, from 1518 his thinking passed quite outside its scope. Preoccupied with God's almighty initiative and man's powerlessness, he was not impressed by the mental techniques through which the mystics sought to ascend the ladder of perfection to the higher states. Unlike theirs, his theology had no pantheist overtones and was altogether Christocentric. He would not follow the mystics into a passive abandonment before their sense of the vast and cloudy infinity of God. For Luther the tragic and triumphant sacrifice of Jesus—seen in all its spiritual and physical terrors—is central to the redemption and hence to all the religious thinking of men. The abstract, impersonal, unintellectual optimism of the *devotio* he replaced by a *theologia crucis* involving a profound anguish both for Christ and for each man chosen to follow him along the way of the Cross.

When we have followed Luther's growth through the lecture-courses of 1509–18, the disputes of 1519, the classics of 1520, we see him as a creative biblical theologian who operated on a broad front in the light of the principle 'holy Scripture is its own interpreter'. His teaching on justification by faith was Pauline and Augustinian, yet it was something more because it came from the depth of a soul which believed itself to have been snatched from the brink of the abyss by the strong arm of Christ alone. Until 1518 it was theologically neither novel nor outside the mainstreams of patristic and medieval theology, a fact fully documented by some of Luther's severest modern Catholic critics. But in 1518 Luther's justificatory concept advanced beyond that of Augustine. He now saw justification not simply as the gradual cleansing of the believer by divine grace, but in the first place as an instantaneous act, whereby the believer appropriates the righteousness earned by Christ. He receives through faith the unmerited imputation of Christ's work and victory. This interpretation of St Paul gave Luther a new joy and confidence; it brought relief to the spiritual suffering only partially assuaged by the counsels of Staupitz. It helped him to close the terrifying gap between the unutterable majesty of God and the miserable inadequacy, the self-centredness, the 'incurving' of man. It came in answer to his terrible vision of Christ the Judge, who might not, despite all his mercy to mankind in general, prove gracious to Luther. From this agonizing predicament he claims to have been rescued as he read *Romans* and came to a new understanding of the text 'The just shall live by faith'. 'Here', he comments, 'I felt that I was altogether born again and had entered paradise itself through open gates.'

Luther's justificatory scheme could also claim a general support from the Gospels: the condemnations of pharisaic observance-religion, the parables of the Labourers in the Vineyard and of the Prodigal Son. But it finds its sharpest definitions in *Romans*, and in certain passages of *Galatians*, *Ephesians* and *Hebrews*. Such passages dwell upon the utter failure of Israel to attain justification—a right relationship with God—by the Mosaic law, by its own works and

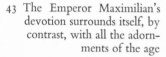

42 Dürer's wood-cut (1510) of the flagellant, in the pietist atmosphere typical of the late Middle Ages, evidences a new attention to the human physique

43 The Emperor Maximilian's devotion surrounds itself, by contrast, with all the adornments of the age

observances, by human righteousness in general. On the contrary, men are justified and saved only by God's bestowal of faith in Christ: 'For by grace are ye saved by faith; and that not of yourselves; it is the gift of God: not of works, lest any man should boast'. Luther was anything but a fundamentalist; he did not attach equal importance to every text. He boldly called *Romans* 'the most important document in the New Testament', and he brushed aside the *Epistle of St James*, with its counter-emphasis upon good works, as 'an epistle of straw'. And by faith he understood no mere intellectual assent to the creeds of the Church, but rather *fiducia*, the sinner's mental attitude of childlike trust as he reached for the saving hand of the Redeemer. Above all, Luther sought to shatter the complacent man-made morality which awards a person credit-points in heaven for every good deed done, every coin in the box, every Mass heard.

57

The less comfortable consequence of this abandonment of celestial accountancy had been foreseen by St Paul before Augustine and Bradwardine, Luther and Calvin embroidered on the theme of predestination. If God, wholly unprompted by pitiful human merit, willed to save some undeserving men from the crowd of the undeserving, then there would seem to remain no effective scope for the exercise of free will. Luther bade men conceive of God as a being infinitely vaster and more mysterious than the God of current anthropomorphism. God extends far beyond the miniature critiques of human reason. Man is too small to question the divine purposes of the masked God; he must accept this omnipotent, overwhelming will, grateful at least that once, in Christ, the mask has been raised and the underlying face of mercy revealed.

Whether or not such concepts were anti-Catholic, they were certainly anti-Aristotelian and anti-humanist. Presently they brought Luther into conflict with Erasmus, who as a good humanist believed in the basic dignity and goodness of man, in man's ability by the exercise of free will to contribute towards his own salvation. In 1525 Luther accordingly directed his *Bondage of the Will* against Erasmus in particular and humanist Christianity in general. He did not, of course, discourage good works or preach antinomianism. Though works availed not a jot towards salvation, they must be done out of love for God and to subdue the flesh. Moreover, he urges, 'faith is always and incessantly in action, or else it is not faith'. He could not understand how people could conceive of the one without the other.

Alongside solifidianism and predestination, Luther enlarged a third doctrine, that of the Word, the self-revealing action of God, whereby the redeeming work of Christ is made known to man. Whatever Luther's left-wing critics may have said, his Word of God did not simply mean the Bible. He and his followers often regard it as threefold: the heard word of preaching; the visible word of the two Gospel sacraments; the written word of the Scriptures, seen and interpreted as a whole.

Around these major concepts revolved Luther's creative theology. His doctrine of the eucharist, misleadingly called consubstantiation,

44 Luther commends the simplicity of the reformed sacrament (left) while consigning the Roman rite to Gehenna

was fully consonant with his teaching of the Word. It involved a real presence in the elements of bread and wine, but this was qualified by a belief in the ubiquity of Christ's glorified body, thus meeting the Zwinglian objection that Christ's body could not simultaneously be in heaven and on earth. From the first Luther strove to distinguish his real presence from that of the Catholics. In his *Babylonian Captivity of the Church*, he dates transubstantiation from the Lateran decree of 1215 and claims that the term and the idea were unknown 'until the false philosophy of Aristotle took root'. He also argues that transubstantiation has proved useless as a safeguard against idolatry, 'because the laity have never understood philosophical hair-splitting about substance and accidents, nor if they were taught it, could they understand it'. He can see no reason to suppose that the 'substance' of the bread ceases to exist at the moment of consecration:

'Why could not Christ maintain his body within the substance of the bread as truly as within its accidents? Iron and fire are two substances which mix together in red-hot iron in such a manner that every portion contains both iron and fire. Why cannot the glorified body of Christ be similarly found in every part of the substance of the bread?'

59

Luther then continues to denounce Aristotelian curiosity and bids his readers 'hold to Christ's words in simple faith'. Nevertheless in 1528 he further developed his own doctrine in the *Confession concerning the Lord's Supper* and thenceforth he maintained it in a spirit as authoritarian as that of Rome. He would not bear with the Zwinglians, when at the Marburg Colloquy of 1529 they could acknowledge only a symbolic character—as distinct from a real presence—in the sacrament. On this most involved and hazardous issue the two movements fell apart. During the half-century following Luther's revolt a huge amount of ingenuity was expended by all parties in order to define the precise metaphysic implied by Jesus at the Last Supper, and in 1577 Christopher Rasperger was able to publish at Ingolstadt a book called *Two Hundred Interpretations of the Words: This is my Body*. However boldly Luther had defined the issues of justification and salvation, he had done nothing to clear the air on this equally polemical matter.

THE REVOLT AND ITS MANIFESTOES

The doctrine of unearned justification through a Christ-given faith could claim little intellectual novelty, yet its literal adoption entailed many practical and subversive results. The array of pious observances, utterances and cash-transactions, the 'doctrine of cheap grace', it equated with the unavailing law of the scribes and Pharisees. The purchase of pardons, prayers and tribute to saints, the multiplication of requiem Masses, the rigours of monasticism and bodily mortification: all these had to go, carrying with them the host

45 This printed receipt of indulgence (*ablasszettel*) was delivered to two brothers at Einsiedeln, December 1521, by a Benedictine monk. Similar forms for confession are also found among the earliest examples of printing

of endowments and institutions to which they had given birth. And here in justice to both sides we may recall that forty years later the Council of Trent itself did at least prune this luxuriant forest. When Luther chose to challenge the Papacy over Tetzel's indulgence-campaign, he found a doctrine of dubious authenticity being abused by fund-raising officialdom in a manner repugnant to many Catholics from Ximenes downwards.

We have already observed the plan of 1514 to promote the youthful Albert of Brandenburg to the see of Mainz and the enormous sum owed by him to Rome. In order to produce this money, it had been arranged to preach in Germany a large-scale indulgence for the rebuilding of St Peter's, half the proceeds to go to Albert and his financial agents, the House of Fugger. And while Albert complied with official doctrine by including the phrase *corde contritus et ore confessus* in his commissions, a less attractive impression was given by the continual presence of the Fugger accountant and by the oratorical extravagances of Tetzel, a hard-bitten trouper who should have known better, for he had been engaged in this type of work at least since 1502. According to a witness at the St Annaberg mines:

'It is incredible what this ignorant and impudent friar gave out. He said that if a Christian had slept with his mother, and placed the sum of money in the pope's indulgence chest, the pope had power in heaven and earth to forgive the sin, and if he forgave it, God must do so also. . . . Item, so soon as the coin rang in the chest, the soul for whom the money was paid would go straightway to heaven.'

46 An anonymous caricature of Johann Tetzel, the commissioner of the great German indulgence of 1517 who provoked the ninety-five theses of Luther. The last lines of his notorious jingle read:
As soon as gold in the basin rings,
Right then the soul to heaven springs

We have in fact Tetzel's instructions and sermon-notes for the parish priests whose help he expected: they leave no doubt as to that perversion of the doctrine of indulgences, for which he was later disgraced. Though Luther still accepted papal authority when he compiled his *Ninety-five Theses*, the matter could hardly have been prevented from compromising the Papacy. It was no mere German scandal, for the ultimate destination of the proceeds proclaimed the real seat of the responsibility. In the familiar quarrels which led to Luther's defiance of the Emperor at Worms, a very great part of German opinion came over to his side with startling alacrity. The most apparent exceptions were among the officialdom interested in preventing reform and among the Dominicans, who would doubtless have defended their man Tetzel against an archangel, had the latter worn an Augustinian habit.

Luther's adversaries were favoured in that they found in the new Emperor Charles V a highly responsible yet callow young man surrounded by imperceptive advisers. When time was still young the Imperial government failed to use Luther's popularity in order to wrest reforms from the Papacy and to reconstruct the German Church before it broke asunder. Their problem, it must be conceded, was far from straightforward, for the huge international inheritance of Charles had emphasized the profound cleavage between Habsburg dynasticism and the interests of the German people. It has been well said that Charles 'was a Habsburg first, King of Spain next, and only at long last the German Emperor'. His military and financial power arose from his non-German possessions. While believing in the need for Conciliar reform, he feared to risk his situation in Spain and Italy by vigorously leading the Germans against the claims of Rome. But he appears not to have understood the extreme weakness of the anti-reform elements in Christendom. In the early 'twenties, before the hardening of politico-religious parties, there still existed an opportunity for agreed reforms on the basis of an understanding between the princes and a mature, critical and statesmanlike Emperor. Just possibly, the Germans might have been offered a middle way less controversial than Luther's, yet nearer to apostolic Christianity than that of the Medici who sat upon the

47 Charles V in 1526:
portrait by
Jan Cornelisz Vermeyen

papal throne, immobilized by interests more local and traditions more effete than those of the Habsburg Emperor himself.

The obvious justice of Luther's attack on abuses lent weight to the more debatable solifidian and antipapal positions which he afterwards proceeded to adopt. By the time of the Leipzig disputations of 1519 he had repudiated not only papal authority but that of General Councils. In 1520, his literary *annus mirabilis*, he produced his most famous revolutionary manifestoes. *To the Christian Nobility of the German Nation*, significantly written in German, covers with unflagging verve the whole gamut of religious, ecclesiastical and social problems. Here Luther attacks the pomp and pride of the Roman court, the horde of greedy cardinals, papal officials and pluralists, the immunity of priests from secular laws, the papal claims to final interpretation of the Scriptures and to the sole right of calling General Councils. Secular rulers, he maintains, should withhold annates and legal causes from Rome; in effect they should set up independent national churches. Luther would see vows of celibacy abolished, allow monks to leave their orders at will, convert religious houses into schools. 'Our baptism consecrates us all without exception and makes us all priests.' Christian men thus all belong to one estate, though called to fill different offices. Luther also demands the abolition of pilgrimages, the simplification of rites and ceremonies, a

63

An den Christli-chen Adel deutscher Nation
von des Christlichen standes besserung.
D. Martinus Luther

48 Title-page of the first of
Luther's three great tracts of
1520, the least theological and
the most patriotic: vernacular
address *To the Christian
Nobility of the German Nation*

parish poor-law system to end mendicity, a re-examination of the
Bohemian heresy, and the allowance of communion in both kinds
to the Hussite laity. In the universities Luther would drop canon law
from the curriculum while greatly limiting the scope of Aristotelian
logic and philosophy in favour of languages, mathematics and
history. The text of the Bible should be studied without an overlay
of theological manuals. Every town should have a school for girls
as well as for boys; in both the Gospel of Christ should be the central
subject. The concluding passages of this astonishing tractate turn to
the laity and show Luther in the rôle of social-economic reformer.
Here he denounces the gluttony and luxury of the moneyed classes,
together with the taking of interest. He calls for 'a bridle on the
Fuggers and such firms' and suggests that Germans should leave the
overcrowded world of trade to rehabilitate agriculture. His vision
for the new age did not embrace its materialism. In the year 1520,
this was indeed an explosive document, and if Luther had written
nothing else he would still have become a portentous figure.

The papal ban of September 1520 was confronted the following month by Luther's *Babylonian Captivity of the Church*, written in Latin and largely directed to the clergy. Here he reduced the seven sacraments to three but from these he was later to subtract confession, leaving only the Scriptural two, baptism and the eucharist. The resultant non-sacramental concept of matrimony hence involved the possibility of divorce and remarriage if the vows were broken. The *Babylonian Captivity* also contains an attack on the sacrificial character of the Mass, together with a remarkably imaginative passage on baptism as symbolizing man's justification and resurrection. Though counselling patience, it denies the right of pope or bishop 'to impose a syllable of law upon a Christian man without his consent'. This latter sentiment the radicals were soon to take literally and Luther to qualify. Again, though the single human estate and the priesthood of all believers reappear in the *Babylonian Captivity*, Luther already sets up alongside them his proposal for a regular ministry called into being by the community or by a ruler.

Unlike the two other famous tracts, *Of the Liberty of a Christian Man* is a straightforward work of edification: a treatise on the faith which begets no mystical quietism but a new and creative liberty, a participation in the battle and the victory of Christ over sin, death and the Devil. For people attuned to Protestant ideas, this has become one of Luther's most endearing works, for within his terms of reference he could write with the authority and sensitivity of a great spiritual guide.

Bulla contra Erro
res Martini Lutheri
et sequarum.

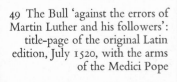

49 The Bull 'against the errors of Martin Luther and his followers': title-page of the original Latin edition, July 1520, with the arms of the Medici Pope

Doctor Oürnar Argentinen. Doctor hock Emser Lipsii Leo papa.r. Antichrist Doctor Eckius Ingelstatensis Doctor Lemp. Tubingensis.

50 (*Above*) Luther's opponents are visual puns: Murner of Alsace, Emser of Leipzig, Pope Leo X, Eck of Ingolstadt and, far right, Lemp of Tübingen, where the caricature appeared about 1525

51, 52 (*Above left*) Luther triumphant over a fallen Thomas Murner, the serpent in a monk's cowl: frontispiece of an attack on the presumptuous *Murnerus Leviathan*, 1521. (*Above right*) Luther humiliated by Murner who, accepting the handicap of the pun on his name, issued in 1522 a stinging indictment of *The Great Lutheran Fool* and his supposed opportunism

53 (*Left*) Philip Melanchthon, 1523, by Cranach the Elder: a counterpoise to the technique of scabrous abuse seen above

54 (*Opposite*) The Cardinal, reversed, becomes a fool: anonymous coloured wood-cut

GERMANY IN TURMOIL

Luther was essentially a professor of biblical theology and a religious revivalist: however fervently he hoped that a reformed Church would uplift society, he was no political planner and confined himself to the task which he believed God had laid on his shoulders. He could not shape the practical outcome of his own amazingly effective propaganda. From his great moment of defiance at Worms and his sabbatical year in the Wartburg, his cause became ever more deeply entrammelled by political intrigue, by rival prophets, by threats of social revolution. During the Wartburg months, as he quietly worked on his famous translation of the Bible, the pamphlets swiftly spread his teaching to millions of receptive readers and hearers. The print-makers accompanied them by a torrent of politico-religious cartoons and caricatures. At the other extreme there appeared Philip Melanchthon's *Loci Communes*, an orderly and academic presentation of the new theology by the young professor of Greek at Wittenberg, who brought all the historical and linguistic techniques of humanism to the service of the cause.

How heavily charged with emotion the German mind had now become we can sense in the agonized entries made in his diary by Albrecht Dürer on hearing a report of Luther's imprisonment:

'I do not know whether he is still alive or was murdered. . . . O all ye pious Christians, join with me in heartfelt mourning for this man, inspired by God. Pray God that another may be sent in his place, as enlightened as he. O Erasmus of Rotterdam . . . see how the filthy tyranny of worldly might and the powers of darkness prevail! Hearken, knight of Christ, ride at the Lord's side, defend the truth and grasp the martyr's crown.'

The mis-casting of Erasmus is not the least significant aspect of this utterance. A most un-Erasmian excitement already manifested itself during the Diet of Worms, Luther being escorted there by knights and entertained in a series of civic receptions. The papal agent Aleander bewailed the vociferous partisanship of the common people at Worms, where Lutheran pamphlets circulated under the nose of the Emperor, and where Aleander found himself forced to bribe the printers and translators in order to get his own work done. In the background lurked the leaders of the knightly party, Franz von Sickingen and Ulrich von Hutten, who despatched violent letters of encouragement to Luther and announced the formation of a league of four hundred knights to combat the papists. Yet various factors prevented the knights from playing a crucial rôle. They lacked statesmanlike leadership, while their indigence compelled them to exploit the peasantry and so prevented them from organizing a politico-religious movement within rural society. Again, in the Swabian League of southern rulers the knights confronted the mightiest force of order in all Germany. In 1522–3 they failed miserably in their attempt to challenge the princes in arms and were swept off the chessboard of the Empire. During the subsequent two years the peasants also tried conclusions with the princes and suffered a like political fate. While some peasants found inspiration in the libertarian phrases of Luther and other religious leaders, this type of outgrowth from economic discontent formed no novelty in the social annals of Germany. Before Luther was born, peasants had been forming *Bundschuh* leagues and listening to local millenarian prophets like Hans Böhm, who back in 1476 had been burned by the Bishop of Würzburg for teaching Christian communism and fostering revolution.

55 A knight is surrounded by the peasants under the banner of the *Bundschuh* or Peasant League: an image of the outburst of 1524–25. The wood-cut is by Hans Weiditz, from Petrarch's *Trostspiegel*, Augsburg, 1532 (see 34 above)

56 Peasants plundering a South German monastery, 1525. Less iconoclastic than acquisitive, they pull fish from the pond, unload sacks of flour from the monks' store; the leaders feast in the refectory while others tipple in the courtyard

MÜNTZER AND CARLSTADT

The years immediately following Worms saw a new resurgence of millenarianism in various parts of Europe, and some of its prophets inevitably had success in canalizing popular economic grievances into religious channels. Of such prophets, the most remarkable was the Saxon priest Thomas Müntzer (*c.* 1490–1525), who had absorbed the traditions of Joachim of Fiore and Tauler, passed through a phase of discipleship to Luther, and finally emerged as arch-critic of the Wittenberg Reformer, whom he called a *Schriftgelehrter* (scribe), a soft-liver and a truckler to authority. Though he displayed a remarkable knowledge of the Bible, Müntzer was at bottom a Spiritualist, believing in direct revelations, visions and dreams. He also introduced into the German radical tradition a species of natural theology. He believed that simple people could be taught the Gospel in Christ's own manner from the book of nature, and that the man-animal relationship had significant analogies with the God-man relationship. This latter poetic (but ultimately macabre) parallel he had almost certainly derived from the *Theologia Naturalis* of Raymond de Sabunde, the early fifteenth-century Franciscan later immortalized by Montaigne. After joining in the confused revivalism at the troubled town of Zwickau, Müntzer went to Prague and tried in vain to raise the Bohemians. He thence made his way back to Saxony and found a hospitable base at Allstedt, where he attracted attention by remodelling Mass, matins and evensong. Increasingly he talked social revolution, seeking to bind workmen and miners into associations pledged to hasten by force the coming of the New Jerusalem. In July 1524 he preached a blood-curdling sermon before Duke John of Saxony, urging that ruler to take up arms against the ungodly. Compelled to resume his travels, Müntzer became deeply involved in the Peasants' Revolt and on its collapse at Frankenhausen in May 1525 he was captured, tortured and put to death.

The other outstanding extremist of the early 'twenties was Luther's senior colleague in the University of Wittenberg, Andreas Carlstadt (*c.* 1480–1541), who not long before Frankenhausen had managed to detach himself from the rebel cause and to escape from Rothenburg in true apostolic fashion by being lowered secretly from the city wall. This learned muddler had already illustrated the hazards presented by enthusiasm to the Protestant movement. A leading defender of Luther in the Leipzig disputations against Eck, he had virtually assumed control in Wittenberg while his leader lay in the Wartburg. Carlstadt there attempted to force the pace by becoming more Lutheran than Luther; he sought to fuse the latter's teachings with mystical elements and with a species of Old Testament puritanism which denounced pictures, images and church music. He also concerted plans for an all-German liturgy, while his affected glorification of simple peasant wisdom involved him in quarrels with his university associates. At Wittenberg the period of Luther's absence had been further enlivened by the appearance of the weaver-prophets from Zwickau, whose patriarchal beards, quaint garb and talk of heavenly visions captivated not merely Carlstadt but some of the steadier lieutenants. Luther's force of character, the power of his preaching, his robust shrewdness on essentials, are all wonderfully illustrated by the speed with which, though little aided by authority, he settled Carlstadt's bear-garden on his return to Wittenberg in the spring of 1522.

57 Thomas Müntzer: engraving   58 Andreas Bodenstein von Carlstadt:
by Christoffel van Sichem, 1609   anonymous contemporary metal-cut

Whatever may be thought of Carlstadt's doctrines, the remainder of his career tends to support Luther's judgement on his character. Not long after leaving Wittenberg he established close contact with Müntzer, while in August 1524 Luther conducted a preaching-tour of the Saale Valley to allay the effects of their extremist teachings. It was at Jena that he came up with his former friend and in the Black Bear tossed him a golden guilder, the traditional challenge to scholarly combat. Luther soon followed this gesture with his entertaining tractate *Against the Heavenly Prophets*. He nevertheless gave his antagonist asylum in his home when Carlstadt's life lay in danger through complicity with Müntzer and the peasants. During the 'thirties Carlstadt worked in Switzerland as a Zwinglian pastor and even in this more congenial atmosphere he entered into every possible dispute and antagonized his tolerant hosts. He nevertheless exerted strong influences upon Anabaptists like Grebel and Hoffmann, and upon Spiritualists like Denck and Franck. When he died of the plague at Basle, his wife made Luther shudder with an undutiful letter lamenting the needless wanderings and hardships which had made her a crippled wreck while still young. One need not be a fanatical admirer of Luther to think that poor Carlstadt in some measure deserved even this dark epitaph. In the leadership of men, sincerity is never enough.

71

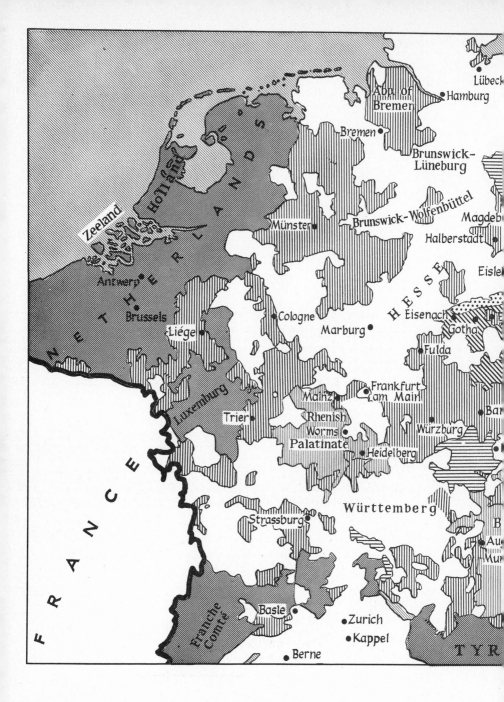

59 Map showing the political divisions in central Europe, 1546

60 Philip, Landgrave of Hesse:
wood-cut by Hans Brosamer,
about 1530

PRINCES AND CITIES

As Müntzer and Carlstadt passed to and fro on their troubled wanderings, as the knights and then the peasants rose and fell, the acceptance of Luther's principles by the German princes and cities brought them into alliance with Electoral Saxony. In 1525 Albert of Hohenzollern, Grand Master of the Teutonic Knights, dissolved his Order, secularized its lands and accepted Lutheranism in his dukedom of Prussia. The following year the young Landgrave Philip of Hesse led his territory into the evangelical camp and he thenceforth represented the spirit which placed militant alliances before niceties of doctrine. In 1528 the Lutherans were joined by the Margrave of Brandenburg-Ansbach, the Count of Mansfeld, the Duke of Schleswig and the Duke of Brunswick. These rulers formed the core of that evangelical minority which in the summer of 1530 faced the Emperor at the Diet of Augsburg, and which signed the famous Confession drawn up in such reticent terms by Philip Melanchthon. Luther, who for obvious reasons could not attend in person, became agitated by the extreme flexibility with which Philip bargained with the Catholics, but in the event he had nothing to fear, since the most liberal Lutheranism remained far from acceptable to the most accommodating of his opponents. The breakdown of the Augsburg negotiations was followed by the Protestant League of Schmalkalden, by renewed Turkish pressures which immobilized Charles, then by a further period of Protestant expansion greatly aided by the mediatory work of Martin Bucer (1491–1551) in the part-Zwinglian southern cities. In 1534 further states were drawn into the fold by their rulers: Nassau, Pomerania and Württemberg, the last a formidable wedge driven into south-western Germany. Somewhat tardily

Ducal (Albertine) Saxony and Electoral Brandenburg adhered five years later still.

We should not simplify the picture of these Evangelical princes. Their zeal for the cause varied widely; few were devoid of political acumen and all must sometimes have calculated the possible gains as against the hazards. All wanted to rid their territories of papal taxation and jurisdiction; few if any felt unworthy to play the rôle of *summus episcopus* within their territories. In addition, the marked rise of prices, in particular that of military costs, together with the stinginess of their Estates and the relative inflexibility of their revenues, made the secularization of Church properties more attractive to the princes than ever before. On the other hand, several of them were devout enthusiasts and all ran very grave risks in defying the Emperor. Moreover, as we propose to explain in our final chapter, the Lutheran rulers did in the event gain surprisingly little in terms of new revenue from the lands of dissolved monasteries. The still popular notion that the spoils of the Reformation made them autocrats independent of their Estates must now without question be dismissed to the great limbo of textbook fables.

61 The reading of the Augsburg Confession to Charles V, in the Diet of Augsburg, 1530

Whatever the importance of princely initiatives, nothing could be more erroneous than to conceive of Lutheranism as a mere princely religion imposed by monarchs upon cowed or indifferent subjects. The first and most decisive landslide took place in a host of towns and cities, the greatest of which were independent of princely rule. By 1524–5 Luther's disciples held control in Erfurt, Gotha, Magdeburg, Nuremberg, Bremen, Altenburg and a host of smaller places. In Catholic Cologne and at Jena there were strong radical movements owing much to Carlstadt, while at this moment the seemingly allied forces of Zwingli were triumphing at Zürich, those of Oecolampadius at Basle, those of Bucer and Capito at Strassburg. In the early 'thirties Augsburg, Hanover and Frankfurt-am-Main stood among the leading converts, and some two-thirds of the Imperial cities soon came to accept the Reformation in one form or another. These cities did not, it is true, adopt a uniform policy throughout the years of crisis between 1522 and 1555. Their attitudes were strikingly modified by secular traditions and local circumstances; how much so we can illustrate by taking those three notable examples elucidated by Dr Hans Baron.

The great central city of Nuremberg, the exemplar of townsmen throughout Franconia and Swabia, sought passionately to combine the new Lutheran belief with its ancient loyalty to the Emperor and to the constitution of the Empire. Nuremberg's extensive territories

62, 63 The atmosphere of a German city of the Renaissance: scenes of wood-carving, painting, astronomy and music decorate this wood-cut from Hans Sebald Beham's series of

had been bestowed by past emperors, to so many of whom she had shown lavish hospitality. Her commerce, extending throughout all Europe, depended in no small measure on the peace and prestige of the Empire. From about 1470 she had steadily refrained from sectional alliances and from following Strassburg's attempts to refuse imperial taxation when emperors and princes had failed to meet the demands of the cities. On the other hand, Strassburg, destined to play so utterly vital a rôle in the drama of the Reformation, was a frontier city far from the centres of Imperial power. Owing little to Habsburg protection, she had found natural allies within the Swiss Confederation long before so many of her citizens felt the attraction of Zwinglian beliefs. Unlike Nuremberg, she lay in a rich country-side; her commerce and her loyalties could in consequence remain somewhat restricted and provincial. Fiercely German in their attitude towards French aggression, the Strassburgers nevertheless felt little interest in the maintenance of lively Imperial institutions. In short, these two leading cities stood at opposite poles, each pursuing old-established principles with a marked consistency.

When in 1529–30 the Emperor's implacable resolve to uphold Catholicism became apparent, Strassburg under its leader Jakob Sturm became closely involved with Philip of Hesse and the princely militants. While the city continued to give liberal asylum to many extremist Protestants, Sturm fought to keep her out of the

the Seven Planets. The panorama of Augsburg, city of the Fuggers and scene of the Diet and Confession of 1530, was drawn about that time by Georg Seld

Zwinglian orbit, so that this alliance with the Lutheran rulers should not be imperilled. Meanwhile Nuremberg, led by a Protestant-humanist chancellor Lazarus Spengler, forfeited the leadership of the Lutheran cities, withdrew from alliances, strove to remain on friendly terms with the Habsburgs, while yet within her walls striving to preserve Lutheranism by a policy of quiet evasion. The internal debate in Nuremberg happens to be fairly well recorded, and we know that Spengler's political theory—which regarded resistance to the Emperor as sinful and unconstitutional—did not in fact meet with the approval of Andreas Osiander and the local Lutheran theologians. The main pressure to maintain Imperial loyalties came not from them but from the secular jurists of Nuremberg, who argued that city governments derived their powers not directly from God, but by delegation from the Emperor.

Standing apart from both these mighty opposites Augsburg found herself following policies at once less consistent and less dignified. Augsburg's prosperity depended on the new colonial trade of Spain and Portugal, while her great banking families, headed by the Fuggers, had risen to affluence largely through loans made to the Habsburgs in return for various concessions, especially in the Tyrolese and Hungarian mines. Augsburg had thus become immensely more dependent than Nuremberg upon Habsburg good-will, and she never scrupled to go behind the backs of other Protestant cities to extract special economic privileges from the Emperor. Even when, during the 'thirties, pressure from the un-privileged orders drove the city into the Schmalkaldic League, Charles well knew that the great resources of the Augsburg bankers could never be placed at the disposal of the Lutheran princes. And when in 1546 war at last broke out between him and the League, the banking families (which had mostly remained Catholiç) withdrew from Augsburg in order to induce the Emperor to refrain from confiscating their far-flung interests. In this they succeeded, but even the Fuggers, whose loans had preserved the dynasty, could not dissuade Charles from punishing luckless Augsburg.

In these and many other instances the religious problems of the German towns immediately became enmeshed in varied secular interests and traditions. But over and above such factors, the new creed encountered in every municipality a complex series of social tensions. It found patriciates already long experienced in the selection of clergy, the surveillance of morals, the administration of schools, charities and secularized properties. These magistrates often showed themselves only too willing to accept the enlargement of such duties and powers when urged so to do by the Reformers. But below this level of dignity and privilege the situation was calculated to cause Luther and his colleagues the gravest anxieties. Of this age, it is true, we use the modern terminology of class-warfare at great peril to truth. With singularly few exceptions, the sixteenth-century mind accepted social stratification as ordained and necessary. One class did not desire or attempt to liquidate another. Even so, bitterness, resentment and intrigue were at least as endemic in town society as in the countryside. The guilds grappled with the oligarchs for influence upon town councils. The mass of poor, unprivileged journeymen and labourers moved restively in the grip of masters, guilds and city councils. They had at least enough sophistication to link the freedom-phrases of Luther with their own dreams of liberation and greater social justice. Even the rebellious peasants of 1524–5 showed themselves capable of this misapprehension, and something more closely approaching a general class-war might have developed had the unprivileged orders of town and country united under common leadership. The ruling orders were at least spared this fearsome trial of strength. Though working-class groups in several small towns did in fact welcome the insurgent peasantry, the grievances and outlook of the two groups proved disparate and would not permanently coalesce. In Luther's Germany there were higher walls between town and country than in the England of Henry VIII.

LUTHER'S RESPONSE

As his religious doctrine spread abroad, Luther was called upon to formulate a policy for his movement amid all these conflicting groups. At bottom he disbelieved in all human agencies. Faced by a society whose incapacity for heartfelt reformation came to disgust

79

him, he trusted in the unaided power of the Word. A Church of the Word had no business to take the lead in secular affairs. With the utmost clarity he stated that his message concerned not the world, but human souls: to settle the affairs of this temporal life was not his duty but that of secular rulers, who acted not so much on Scriptural principles as upon reason, tradition and equity. As a Church-organizer in a real world Luther was forced to lean upon the princes and their officials. In Electoral Saxony the process became all the easier, because it so happened that the successive Electors of his day were pious men, prepared to take risks for the cause. It has been argued that we find here a prince-worship natural to Luther's *petit bourgeois* upbringing, the typical outlook of a priest whose father had risen by hard effort to the status of a mining-lessee. In this view, the urban middle class, including such small entrepreneurs, lined up under the princes against many common enemies: the Papacy, the bankers, the rebellious peasants, the socialist sectarians. Yet this explanation of Luther's social allegiances remains unverifiable and dogmatic; it certainly seems inadequate to cover his recorded thinking. That he consciously attacked political and social problems from a religious and moral angle cannot be seriously disputed by anyone familiar with his mind and writings. While he believed in the divine right of temporal rulers, he was no blind lackey of German princes and magistrates. If with undue optimism he relied on them to redress their own faults, he often denounced those faults: indeed did ever a man of the people address rulers in the language used by Luther? Moreover, his regard for traditional authority bade him for many years to uphold the Emperor as well as the territorial princes, and until 1530, when his hand was forced, he strove to restrain the latter from preparing armed resistance against their Imperial suzerain. The basis of Luther's position was a profound distaste for the rising tendency to intertwine the functions of Church and State; he hated to see the prince as a heavy-handed *defensor fidei* or the pastor as an invader of secular administration.

Luther's detestable advice to the princes that they should mercilessly slay the peasant rebels reflected the terror of 'responsible' leaders in the face of impending anarchy. However intelligible the

64 The three Saxon Electors: Frederick the Wise (reigned 1486-1525), his brother John the Steadfast and John Frederick (reigned 1532-54: son of the Steadfast), by Cranach the Elder. The gravelly riverine lands around Wittenberg form the background

fears of a religious leader who saw the impending ruin of his work, his historical reputation would have been better served had he silently left this bloody task to the princes, who could be trusted to discharge it with a full measure of harshness. Yet this utterance apart, Luther showed himself far from unmindful of peasant grievances and lordly oppressions. He condemned greed and exploitation wherever he saw them, even though he profoundly believed in the sinfulness of actual rebellion. Whatever his unconscious prejudices, his actual thinking on mundane matters was based on religious principles. His family background, his career in Church and university, the harrowing nature of his spiritual crises, his marked versatility and independence, his wide contacts with all the social orders had made him far less class-conscious than most men of his time. On the other hand, his moral and biblical judgements were usually pervaded by a shrewd sense of the practicalities. And for that matter, what line do his modern critics think he should have taken? No religious programme could be realized without secular order. As a responsible spiritual and ecclesiastical reformer, he would have been insane to pin his faith to Hutten and the knights, still more insane to back the peasant-confederacies, or Müntzer and the hirsute prophets of Zwickau. Being a German and not a Swiss, he could not organize self-sufficient confederations of cities in the face of princely states and absolutist trends. He could rebuke sinners high and low, right and left, but ultimately he could build only upon the platforms erected by more or less evangelical princes and city-oligarchs. In a word, even had Luther turned to politics, there existed no short cut out of sixteenth-century Germany.

81

LATER LIFE

While in some senses the defiance at Worms marked the apogee of Luther's career, he nevertheless remained for another quarter-century a towering figure in the Protestant landscape, an indefatigable preacher, a writer of catechisms and hymns, an original interpreter of the Scriptures, an experimenter in church-administration, a trainer of missionaries. This phase of his career saw nothing less than the reorganization and inspiration of a Church at once threatened by secular greed and yet swiftly ramifying throughout Europe, a Church achieving influence even in countries where it was not allowed to establish its own institutions. To help him accomplish these enormous tasks, Luther enjoyed some remarkable advantages. He never mellowed, it is true, and to his dying day he could still fall victim to attacks of anger, bitterness and depression. To the terrible misgivings of earlier years there was now sometimes added the fear that he might after all have led whole peoples into the abyss of error. Yet he never failed to emerge from these dark hours with his faith and purpose strengthened. With marriage his personal life received settling and humanizing influences. The Luther who wrote a pleasant fairytale for his son, who mourned the loss of a beloved daughter, who talked more sense than his contemporaries about sex and family life, this Luther was no longer the tormented young monk of earlier days. As in the first stages of his revolt he had enjoyed the backing of the Augustinian Order against his Dominican foes, so in his later years he received enthusiastic support from the whole faculty of Wittenberg, whose collective achievement has seldom been fully valued by historians. After Worms Lutheranism was never

65, 66 (*Far left*) The wedding-portraits of Luther and Katherine von Bora, presumed 1525, by Cranach the Elder

67 Georg Burckhard (Spalatin), the Elector's chaplain and Luther's early friend at court, 1537: by Cranach the Elder

in danger of becoming a one-man religion. In Philip Melanchthon he found a lieutenant with intellectual gifts complementary to his own, but one whose work was never so distinguished as when subordinated to the firmer purposes of Luther. He experienced the advantages as well as the burdens of fame and notoriety. To Wittenberg there came between 1520 and 1560 some 16,000 students, about one-third from north Germany, one-third from south Germany and the rest foreigners. Some hundreds of these must have sat and listened at Luther's ever-hospitable board before going forth as active disciples throughout Europe.

Above all Luther had a solid political base in the Saxon Electorate, a state large enough to count in Imperial politics yet not so large as to remain uninfluenced by its leading theologians. Thanks to the early friendship of Georg Spalatin, court chaplain and librarian to Frederick the Wise, he enjoyed from the first the steady support of princes who had no intention of handing him over to the mercy of the Emperor. Meanwhile over the years Charles was time after time thwarted in his efforts to enforce the Imperial ban against Luther, thwarted by the intermittent pressures of France and the Turk, by the hesitation even of Catholic princes to place their forces under his command, by quarrels with Rome itself. And when historians of Lutheranism regret its involvement in political rivalries, they should not forget that the situation throughout Luther's lifetime contributed most favourably to the survival of his cause, and that the real perils arose only in 1546. In the February of that year Luther, exhausted in mind and body, died suddenly when on his winter mission to adjudicate between the disputing Counts of Mansfeld. Even had he lived, he could hardly have pacified the disastrous quarrel then arising from the ambitions of Maurice of Saxony.

To understand the complexities of Luther's character, we should examine his well-documented later life rather than those heavily misted stories concerning his youth. Like most shapers of history, he eludes the simple formula. He contains a bundle of antitheses, which, instead of becoming locked in tension, had a strange habit of resolving into decisions and policies. Within his temperament there lay both a sane, practical, humorous grasp of life and yet a liability to those neurotic phases which have inevitably been labelled manic-depressive by people who fail to understand their necessary and creative character. His writing can show a delicate awareness both of the spiritual and the natural world; it can also show a coarseness and a truculence remarkable even in that polemical age. His theology combines an austere biblicism with a rich fund of original insights, his attitude to men an abiding passion for spiritual liberty with a growing intolerance toward divergent opinions. Lacking the intellectual precision and the polished cosmopolitanism of Calvin, he had other gifts which the great Frenchman could not boast: an impressive spontaneity, a generous interest in people, a vast ability to inspire affection, a disarming frankness and a capacity for self-criticism which was never hypocritical. Despite his scholastic training, his thought lacked neatness and consistency of detail. He spoke and wrote all too bluntly and rashly under the impulses of enthusiasm or indignation. Like most religious leaders of his age he too readily equated his own convictions with the voice of God. But more than any leader he fused together the two revolutionary elements already so observable in the German mind on the eve of his appearance: the element of criticism against the Church, the element of aspiration toward a deeper yet simpler spiritual life.

LUTHER THE WRITER

Luther's impact upon history relates in large part to his career as an author, and this career to his genius for forthright statement in that literary language which he deliberately based on the administrative idiom of the Saxon Chancery. Intelligible to Low Germans and High Germans alike, his works played no small part in the birth of the nation, even while their author was consummating its great spiritual division. A compulsive and most prolific writer, Luther knew how to coin the telling phrase, to construct the paragraph which hammered its way straight into the core of a subject, to introduce the touch of humour or invective which moved the common man. But he became a great popularizer less through conscious artifice than through the sheer force of his own profound and violent convictions.

From the humanists Luther derived rather more than the methods of textual criticism. We are accustomed to view humanism as at once aristocratic and rhetorical, yet in the last resort it contributed as much to normal utterance as to formal oratory. Some of its greatest writers cultivated plain, unscholastic, unpedantic statement in the vernacular, a style which could reach the generality of half-educated readers and in the end a large section of the illiterate populace. Erasmus did not write in Dutch, yet he too bulks large in an age of commonsense prose. This bridging of the gap between intellectuals and a far wider public may also, it is true, derive from earlier traditions of vernacular preaching and from the more popular writers of the *devotio moderna*. But the instrument did not obtain full development until the age of Machiavelli and Luther. The famous translations of the Bible by Luther and by William Tyndale are but specialized examples of this vernacular technique. In the first half of the sixteenth century its penetration into society had been much enhanced, not by the invention of printing alone, but also by an apparently steep rise in the number of literate laymen. In the German cities there were readers and even authors among the tradesmen and manual workers. While Luther rejected the claims of common men to devise theologies or to direct religious movements, he displayed an enormous zeal to reach such men, and he found a mode of expression appropriate to their needs. In the world of Hans Sachs we can observe not a little of Luther's historical significance.

The Weimar Edition of Luther's works, begun in 1883 and likely to be completed about 1970, will include fifty-seven volumes of his original writings, twelve of his work on the German Bible, eleven of his letters and six of the *Table Talk*. Meanwhile a slightly compacter American edition now in progress seeks to translate the whole works in some fifty-five large volumes. It would be absurd to claim that Luther seldom repeated himself, or that he was incapable of writing a dull page. Yet in comparison with most religious writers of his day the points of perennial interest are remarkably frequent. With a generosity which never counted the cost, he poured his mind and his physical health into the composition of this library, for he believed that quantity mattered to the cause. When Martin Bucer of Strassburg somewhat priggishly urged the Wittenberg theologians to get out into the world and preach, Luther replied in the pregnant words: 'We do that with our books.' He knew his century.

68, 69 Lutheran title-pages: the *Great Catechism* (1529) for adults, part of the first systematic literature for religious education; and the first complete German Bible (1534), on which Luther worked for a decade

70 Luther and his collaborators: from the right, Melanchthon, Caspar Cruciger, Justus Jonas and, oddly at this date, Erasmus. Bugenhagen is next to Erasmus; Spalatin and Johann Förster (bearded) are behind Luther.

SCANDINAVIA

However moderately couched, the Confession of Augsburg (1530) marked the definitive break of the Lutheran states with Rome and with the Habsburgs. It also clearly parted company from Zwingli and showed lesser divergences between Wittenberg and the Protestant movement in south-western Germany, led by the mediating Bucer. Despite this hardening of its dogmatic arteries, Lutheranism had by no means acquired that complacency which began to affect it not long after Luther's death. It still retained a great potential for expansion, based upon positive and genuine religious attractions, upon popular anticlericalism and upon the worldly advantages which it offered to various elements among the governing classes. Again, Lutheranism appealed to German nationalism even more than the Papacy appealed to Italian nationalism. Its expansion outside Germany depended to a conspicuous extent upon the support of the patriotic German communities in the trading cities of northern and eastern Europe. Throughout Scandinavia and the eastern Baltic, Hanseatic influences had become far more concrete than those of Catholic Rome, which inspired mild conservatism rather than impassioned defence.

Perhaps as early as 1522 Herman Tast was preaching the Evangelical religion at Husum in Schleswig. The monk Hans Tausen, the so-called Danish Luther, spent eighteen months in Wittenberg, returned in 1525 and openly preached it at Viborg the following year. Danish Bibles compiled by order of the deposed King Christian II, another recent visitor to Wittenberg, also furthered the movement. By 1527 it had virtually broken the connections of the Danish Church with Rome. King Frederick I refused to persecute Lutherans, permitted clerical marriage and by 1530 had begun to alienate the monastic lands. Six years later Christian III, having won his fight for the crown, continued the policy of secularization by way of paying

his war-debts. The Lutheran bishops henceforth had to resign themselves to becoming salaried officials. The Church ordinance of 1537, approved by Luther and closely supervised by his emissary Johann Bugenhagen, established a truly national Church. Danish Lutheranism produced bishops in its own idiom, notably its great organizer Peder Palladius, Bishop of Zeeland, who along with Hans Tausen gave it sound literary and administrative foundations. Meanwhile in Norway a German monk had in 1526 introduced the new teachings to the German colony at Bergen. Norwegian conformity with the Danish pattern was sealed a decade later by the subjugation of the country to the crown of Denmark. Here, however, Catholicism lingered more tenaciously; the Bible was not at first translated into Norwegian, while the Lutheran movement appeared too obviously a vehicle for Danish overlordship.

In Sweden the Catholic bishops under Hans Brask of Linköping proved stronger than in Denmark, while outside German-dominated Stockholm a popular Protestantism was created only with difficulty. The fate of the evangelical religion hung in no small measure upon the decisions of King Gustavus Vasa, during whose long reign (1523–60) the power of the crown and the influence of Protestantism advanced in close conjunction. From tentative origins there grew at last that solid Lutheran monarchy which a century later took the

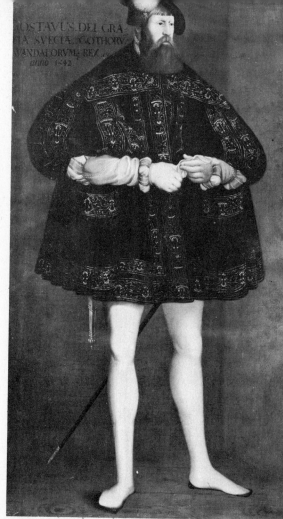

71 (*Far left*) Christian II of Denmark, 1523, by Cranach the Elder

72 (*Above*) Gustavus Vasa enthroned (left) hears dispassionately the pleading of the city of Stockholm; at the rear of his mercenary army (right) he prepares to take the city (1523) founding the new and more powerful Swedish state which adopted Lutheranism

73 (*Right*) Gustavus Vasa in 1542

74 View of Stockholm in 1535

centre of the European stage and saved German Protestantism from Habsburg reconquest. The chief adviser of Gustavus Vasa was Laurentius Andreae, archdeacon of Strängnäs, who began a conservative programme of reforms based on the authority of the Bible and on the public ownership of church property under royal management. Olavus Petri, who had been alongside Luther at Wittenberg as early as 1516–18, used a preaching appointment in Stockholm from 1524 to inculcate the new doctrines. Along with Andreae, he seems to have been responsible for the first Swedish translation of the New Testament, which appeared in 1526, the same year as Tyndale's English equivalent. It was closely based upon the Strassburg edition of Luther's translation and upon the Greek and Latin versions by Erasmus. Meanwhile German pamphlets flowed into Sweden from Königsberg, whence Duke Albert of Prussia also sent envoys to advise Gustavus, especially on the eve of the momentous Diet of Västerås.

Having called this assembly in the summer of 1527 with a view to solving his financial and ecclesiastical problems, the King was faced by strong conservative opposition from Bishop Brask and the nobility. By the threat of abdication he nevertheless brought the Diet to the point of transferring much ecclesiastical property to the crown and some to the nobles. In the end the Diet also permitted the free preaching of Lutheranism in Sweden, with toleration for both Catholics and Protestants so long as they preached 'the pure Word of God' from the Gospels. The rest of the reign was marked by the steady progress of the new faith in the face of sporadic popular resistance, by the total secularization of Church lands, the development of a Swedish liturgy, an enterprising programme of evangelical education, and an immense spate of writing from the pens of Olavus Petri and his brother Laurentius. The latter, who became archbishop of Uppsala in 1531, fostered the progress of the Swedish Reformation until his death in 1573. Shortly before the latter date he promulgated a series of Church ordinances which illustrate the flexible character of expanding Lutheranism. Accepting the Bible as the sole guide to faith, this code avoided any idolatry toward Luther and accorded equal weight to those modifications lately introduced by the party under Melanchthon. The Swedish bishops received a measure of independence; they were to be chosen by clergy and laity but confirmed by the King, parish priests being appointed by their congregations.

While in Sweden Lutheranism created at last an impressive national Church, its influence passed well beyond the bounds of religion. Throughout the Reformation decades, the translation of the Bible and the large output of evangelical writing provided the very foundations of modern Swedish literature. As a moulder of national cultures, the Reformation can claim an even greater place in Scandinavian history than in that of the Protestant western nations. Even today it is still possible to feel how fully Lutheranism once comprehended these societies, whereas Anglicanism never comprehended the more complex social and cultural forms of England. In Sweden's political dependency Finland, the evangelical religion also figured dramatically in the annals of literature. Its leader Archbishop Michael Agricola (*c.* 1510–57) is the acknowledged father of written Finnish, a language wholly separate in origin and structure from its Teutonic and Slavonic neighbours. Like the Danish and Swedish leaders, he exemplifies the true Lutheran pattern of versatile and indefatigable writing for the ever-active presses. Yet while Agricola's translation of the New Testament was not printed until 1548, Lutheran doctrine had been preached at Turku since the mid-'twenties and at Viipuri before 1530. Ideas moved with surprising rapidity across the Baltic trade-routes, yet they were usually modified on arrival by local requirements and personalities. Though Agricola studied at Wittenberg in 1536–9, his conservative programme suggests no servile imitation of Saxon models. His doctrine of purgatory, his great reverence for the Virgin Mary, his continuance of pre-Reformation emphases on the Passion and on the Eucharist, his retention even of the controversial feast of Corpus Christi: all these backward-looking characteristics were balanced by a profound biblicism and a sense of pastoral responsibility stemming from the new order. In Finland the change from late medieval piety to conservative evangelicalism was thus carried through with an enviable freedom from iconoclasm, polemical abuse and martyrdoms.

EASTERN EUROPE

Elsewhere in Europe, Lutheranism encountered political and social conditions less favourable than those of Scandinavia. Moreover, while knocking at doors or winning precarious places on thresholds, it was soon overtaken by new visitors—Zwinglianism, Anabaptism, Calvinism—making rival claims to admission. In regard to the prior circumstances we can draw sharper distinctions between eastern and western Europe than between the west and Scandinavia. The three eastern kingdoms of Poland, Hungary, and Bohemia, all at first under branches of the Jagiellon dynasty, were no mere frontier-provinces but integral members of European civilization. Though Poland contained Orthodox groups in Lithuania and Galicia, the confrontation of these kingdoms by the Turk and by the Orthodox Church had at first strengthened their loyalty to Catholicism. On the other hand, the tax-exemption of the immensely rich Polish clergy, together with the severities of the Church courts, gave rise to virulent anticlericalism on the part of the nobles both before and during the years of the Reformation. All three countries, especially Poland, were now absorbing powerful Italian and humanist influences upon scholarship, literature, art and architecture. At Cracow alone from 1503 to 1536 some 294 works were printed—more than in the whole of England. Here also fine Renaissance buildings spread around the court of Sigismund I and his queen Bona Sforza (m. 1519), while the universities of Prague and Cracow were better known throughout Europe than either Oxford or Cambridge.

75, 76 A Polish lady pays a visit to her tailor, and a Cracow wool-merchant checks his stock: early sixteenth-century miniatures

77 Peasants and knights in the Polish granary: detail of the 'Massacre of the Innocents' from the sixteenth-century Jerusalem Triptych, Warsaw

The progressive response of these kingdoms towards western ideas did not, however, extend to their political and social life. They were now being differentiated from the western and northern states by the weakness of their elective monarchies and by the advancing power of their great territorial nobles. The latter were advancing on two fronts: economically at the expense of their serfs and politically at the expense of their kings. Town-life had developed less markedly than in central and western Europe: particularly in Poland the urban classes consisted to a surprising extent of Germans, who lacked social influence and never acquired the weight to tip the scales in favour of monarchy. The farming of great estates at once multiplied the labour-dues of the peasantry, augmented the wealth of the gentry and made the eastern kingdoms (especially Poland, which was then larger than France and possibly five times as populous as England) the granary for the rising town-populations of central and western Europe. The excessive influence of over-mighty landlords upon the national and provincial Diets withered the sinews of monarchy and bureaucracy at the very moment when the Ottoman threat demanded their strengthening.

In Hungary Lutheranism came upon a disastrous political situation. In 1526 the Jagiellon dynasty and the independence of the greater part of the kingdom came to an end on the bloody field of Mohács. Among the dead were seven of the sixteen Hungarian bishops, whose sees then underwent long and disastrous vacancies. Rival Diets elected two kings: the Emperor's brother Ferdinand, who ruled

93

the western provinces, and John Zápolyai, who held Transylvania and eastern Hungary. From 1541 the Turks permanently occupied a broad wedge of territory between the two, despising but tolerating all forms of Christianity, and allowing missionaries and other travellers easy movement between all three zones. Meanwhile the rival kings, both anxious to win over the nobles and towns, could not afford to be fastidious over religion. These circumstances favoured the incursions of Protestantism. On the other hand, Lutheran propaganda and worship were presented in the German language and the early conquests took place in those towns dominated by German settlers, notably among the large, privileged but unpopular 'Saxon' communities of Transylvania. Conversely the writings of the Swiss Reformers, being in Latin, appealed to educated Hungarians just as to educated Poles, and especially to those already familiar with the literature of humanist reform. Before 1550 Calvinist missionaries began to arrive in person and their success among the Magyar population outstripped that of the Lutherans.

In describing the Hussite heresy, we recognized the great complexity of the Bohemian scene upon which the Lutheran missionaries intruded. A native heresy of this strength could be a repellent as well as an ally, since many Bohemians felt that their own tradition obviated the need for Luther's message. When in 1542 Luther came to an accord with the Bohemian Brethren on the matter of the Eucharist, a certain merging of the streams had begun, especially among the German population, but this did not affect the practices of the great majority. Meanwhile German Anabaptists also arrived and began to make converts.

To Poland Lutheranism came for the most part by the indirect route of the Baltic. In Riga and Reval the strong German elements, led by preachers like the Pomeranian Andreas Knopken, had by 1525–6 forced through evangelical policies amid much iconoclasm and secularization of Church property. From these Baltic places and from Duke Albert's domain in Prussia, German traders and missionaries steadily carried Luther's message into Poland, but not all the factors conspired in their favour. King Sigismund I patronized humanists, yet he began by putting down an evangelical movement in his German subject-city of Danzig. Again, as Polish vernacular literature and Latinism developed under Italian influences, the educated classes showed little disposition to undergo German cultural colonization. At the time of Sigismund's death in 1548 the Lutherans had still made only a limited impression upon this enormous country of independent noblemen and conservative peasants. By this time also, Calvinism had once again entered into successful competition, while ere long certain intellectual Polish aristocrats were to afford hospitality to some of the most 'advanced' religious thinkers in Europe, particularly to the Anti-Trinitarians.

Lutheranism thus spread northward and to a lesser extent eastward along paths made smooth by German traders and by the *diaspora* of German settlements in the trading cities. In some sense it was a ghost of the Hansa and the Teutonic Knights. In contrast, the cities of western Europe were far less heavily dominated by such colonies. In London, for example, the German merchants at the Stilyard ran true to form and in 1526 abolished the Mass at the church assigned to them. But so great a capital under so strong a monarchy was no Reval or Riga; it could not be stampeded by any merchant group and the English ecclesiastical authorities speedily forced some of the Stilyard men to do penance for their heresy.

FRANCE

The origins of French Protestantism are commonly placed in the circle of evangelical humanists and Pauline theologians assembled from 1516 by Briçonnet at Meaux. There the unrepentant Lefèvre produced his French translation of the Scriptures. There too might sometimes be found Guillaume Farel, destined in later years to lay the foundations of Genevan Reform and summon Calvin to erect the edifice. Among their close friends was the young Paris professor Louis de Berquin, converted by Luther's *Theses* and a translator of his writings, an able publicist who might have fused the varied currents of French Protestantism but for his condemnation and burning in 1529. The *Journal of a Paris Merchant* records the popular impression that 'most of Meaux is infected with Luther's false doctrine, and the man called Fabry [*sic*] is the cause of the said confusion'.

On the other hand, when in later years both Calvin and Farel refused to accept the men of Meaux as their precursors, they were not unreasonable. The gentle and versatile Lefèvre did not attack the Papacy or countenance a schism; he lacked the ruthlessness, the single-minded concentration, the marvellous instinct for mass-publicity shown by Luther. Meaux even attracted conservatives like Josse van Clichtove, soon afterwards one of the most effective literary opponents of Luther. By 1523-4 Briçonnet himself was induced to take hostile measures against Lutheranism and within a decade of its origins there no longer existed any chance that the group would form the epicentre of an earthquake within the French Church. Nevertheless, from about 1520 the influence of Luther had become appreciable elsewhere in France, and the very style of the Saxon Reformer is clearly mirrored in the writings of publicists like Farel and Aimé Maigret. Even Rabelais shows himself indebted to Lutheran writings. Great numbers of books by Luther and other Protestant authors, many translated into French, flowed in from Antwerp, Frankfurt, Basle and Strassburg. Before long secret presses came into action in Paris, Lyons, Meaux and Alençon. As early as 1519 the printer Froben told Luther that a consignment of 600 books were *en route* for France and Spain: 'they are sold in Paris; even the doctors of the Sorbonne are reading and approving them'. Certain wills left by members of Catholic families show them also in possession of proscribed books. Alongside this surreptitious trade, many editions of the Bible in French were promoting a change of spirit. Between 1528 and 1546 Robert Estienne alone printed five full editions of the Bible and at least five other volumes of excerpts.

The educated converts were soon followed by large groups of town-artisans, prompted in some places by members of the lower clergy. By the time Lefèvre fled from Meaux (1525) the town itself had a contingent of Protestants; soon afterwards there appeared similar groups at Noyon and Amiens in the north; at Metz, Bar-le-Duc, Châlons-sur-Marne and Vitry in the north-east; at Alençon and elsewhere in Normandy; in the south at Lyons and Grenoble; in Navarre and far scattered across the ancient lands of the Albigenses. In Paris itself a Protestant congregation centred upon the Latin

Quarter. Yet until the arrival of Calvin's missionaries, French Protestantism tended to be diffuse and even individualist; it drew inspiration from a wide variety of sources ranging from Erasmus and Lefèvre, through Luther, Zwingli and Bucer, to the Anabaptists. The term *luthérien* was employed most imprecisely and many of the heretics persecuted under it were in fact sectarians of various sorts. Louis de Berquin, the most aristocratic and distinguished of its martyrs, could hardly be regarded as typical of French heresy.

These beginnings of French Protestantism were not unimpressive, but many factors inhibited its growth. The implacable hostility of the Sorbonne and the Parlement de Paris did much to control the new beliefs in the centre which might most easily have got out of hand. It suited Francis I to support the Lutheran princes in his struggle against Charles V and for a time French Protestants had great hopes of their king, whose sister Marguérite openly patronized Meaux. Even so, the Crown had gained what it wanted by the Concordat of 1516; it now relied on the French Church and on the Parlement for financial and constitutional support. Francis himself was seldom infected by moral fervour. Unlike his rival Henry VIII he had no strong personal reasons for quarrelling with Rome and unlike the Germans his subjects did not think France the milch cow of the Papacy. In these years the tide of loyalty still ran high and Francis had not to face the rivalry of great territorial princes like those who backed Luther. The social structure of France did not easily lend itself to permeation by Lutheran influences. Here as elsewhere, Protestantism flourished best among townsmen, yet the French towns contained no large minorities of Teutons and did not form parts of the German economic network. In general, even the larger French cities at this date lacked both the political and the spiritual independence of their Imperial and Swiss counterparts. Meanwhile the peasants clung to their old saints and pious observances. Urban life did not dominate the huge agrarian society of France, which remained largely feudal and rather slow to respond to the stimulus of intellectuals, whether native or foreign. Again, despite the Concordat and despite an incapacity for united and independent action, the French Church remained capable of a

97

CLes chosescontenues en
ce present liure.

CVne epistre exhortatoire.

La S.Euangile selon S.Matthieu. б. i.
La S.Euangile selon S.Marc. i. ii.
La S.Euangile selon S.Luc. n.Bi.
La S.Euangile selon S.Jehan. p. ii.

CAucunes annotations. L. i.

CHRISTVS DICIT
MARCI XVI.

Praedicate Euangelium omni crea-
turae.Qui crediderit.& ba-
ptisatus fuerit: sal-
uus erit.
1633

Cum priuilegio.
1667

78 Francis I as humanist patr▪
with Erasmus (left) and Albe▪
Pio, Count of Carpi and the
Valois Ambassador to Rome

79 (*Above*) Title-page of the
French New Testament of
Jacques Lefèvre d'Étaples, firs▪
edition of June 1923: issued
under the protection of the
Queen Mother Louise of Sav▪
and the King's sister, Marguér▪
d'Angoulême

vigorous local and regional self-defence. By the late 'twenties, several
of its provincial councils were attempting reforms and persecuting
heretics, while many French bishops still wielded great influence
within their dioceses. For all these reasons no violent swing to heresy
occurred, and when at last the Crown threw its forces into the battle,
the first phase was bound to end in a Catholic victory.

It seems characteristic of the superficiality of Francis that a personal
affront should have decided his policy. This turning-point came in
1534, when in Paris and other cities there appeared a rash of printed
placards attacking the Catholic doctrine of the Mass. An indiscreet
Protestant having fixed one of these to the door of the royal bed-
room at Amboise, the King took mortal offence and authorized
widespread persecution. Though he did not steadily maintain this

98

pressure, it was renewed at the end of the reign with a massacre of some 3,000 Waldensians in Provence and the execution of numerous Protestant artisans at Meaux. By this time, however, the new force of Calvinism had begun to operate in France and it was to prove a match for that more enthusiastic royal persecutor, King Henry II.

ITALY, THE NETHERLANDS, ENGLAND

Sixteenth-century Spain experienced Erasmian reformism on the one hand and scattered heresies on the other, but it did not see an organized Lutheran movement. Even in Italy early Protestantism had an insecure and sporadic character. It found a large part of the country already subjected to Spain and even in the Venetian lands the old secularist antipapalism had little in common with the antipapalism of Luther. Again, the Catholic reforms already current in the religious orders had begun to absorb spiritual energies which might otherwise have turned into less orthodox channels. Amongst Italians intellectual curiosity tended to weigh more heavily than religious emotion. As early as 1519 a bookseller at Pavia was selling works by Luther and Melanchthon as a commercial venture, while about the same time Melanchthon was studied by Roman citizens

80 The harbour and town of Antwerp, about 1540, by an anonymous Antwerp master

and even by officials of the papal Curia. It is certain that within a few years Lutheran views were widely and seriously discussed throughout Italy, though as in France authority tended to use the term Lutheran of any heretic. This position became no simpler when the Waldensians allied first with the Zwinglians, then with the Calvinists.

In Venice, such great importance was attached to trading with Germany that the government showed a marked reluctance to deal with the many heretics who had come from beyond the Alps. Another centre was the court of Ferrara, to which Renée of France came as Duchess in 1528, and where she harboured Protestants of various schools. Her circle appears, however, to have been a place of refuge rather than the headquarters of a missionary religion. In Naples from 1534 the celebrated devotional writer Juan de Valdés (c. 1500–41) built up another aristocratic coterie capable of dangerously free speculations, one which attached far more importance to religious experience than to ecclesiastical authority. Though Valdés never left the Church, some of his associates did so under sensational circumstances. One was no less a figure than Bernardino Ochino, Vicar-General of the Capuchins, who fled in 1541 to Geneva, became a Lutheran, worked at Augsburg, Canterbury and Zürich, went on to Poland and died (1564) in Moravia. Another associate of Valdés was the Augustinian Pietro Martire Vermigli (1500–62), familiar to us in England as Peter Martyr. Though called a Lutheran, he accepted the new doctrines at Naples chiefly through his study of Bucer and Zwingli. Escaping from Italy in 1542, he occupied a professorship with Bucer at Strassburg, came to England five years later with Ochino, served as Regius Professor at Oxford, was imprisoned for a time by Queen Mary, and ended his days at Zürich in assiduous correspondence with his Anglican friends. A number of Franciscan, Augustinian and Carmelite friars in Italy developed strong affinities with Lutheranism. As wandering preachers they were hardly amenable to episcopal discipline; in Italy as in Germany and England a good many of them stood at the forefront of the Reformation. Amid all these enthusiasts, Italian Protestantism remained individualist rather than institutional. Though immensely curious and fond of experiment, the Italian mind continued to resist Teutonic emotional and ecclesiastical patterns. And in the last resort, the Italian princes and cities, living alongside the Papacy and the pro-consuls of Spain, could hardly afford the luxury of public experimentation with religion. Had they made the attempt, the Spaniards would not have sanctioned in Italy the system *cujus regio, ejus religio*.

While in Switzerland the Lutheran movement merged with Zwinglianism, or was suffocated by it, in the Teutonic Netherlands its chances seemed distinctly brighter. In particular the great cosmopolis of Antwerp had a strong German community, numerous printing presses and a traditional independence of outlook. Nevertheless its sovereign the Emperor Charles soon showed a hostile hand. The most Netherlandish of the Habsburgs, he was continuing with success the centralizing policy of the Burgundian princes. He steadily strengthened and lengthened the arm of his government at Brussels, to what effect his triumph of 1541 over rebellious Ghent was to show. Unlike central and northern Germany, the Low Countries lay under his personal lordship and here he had no reason to play a waiting game with heresy. From the moment he promulgated the first papal bull against Luther in Brussels, he was busy issuing a stream of edicts and erecting a system of inquisitors to support the Catholic bishops. As early as 1523 his government burned two Dutch Augustinians, the protomartyrs of Lutheranism. Luther's already numerous sympathizers in the Netherlands were not merely driven underground, but in many cases driven into the arms of Anabaptism, which burst with such force into the Netherlands during the late 'twenties. Radicals and extremists tend to flourish in proscribed movements, but while this fate at first befell the Netherlandish Reformation, in the longer run Calvinism was to supplant Anabaptism and take the lead in defeating the Habsburg policy of unification.

In England the situation bore certain initial resemblances to that we have witnessed in France. Like Francis I, Henry VIII was a monarch of conservative personal views, enjoying immense loyalty among his subjects and able to protect the English Church at the expense of its subjugation to the royal power. But many other English factors proved unique. Pre-Lutheran heresy was established

81 Title-page of the Great Bible, 1539.
King Henry VIII (top) presents copies to
Cranmer (left) and Cromwell, who
distribute them to priests and people,
inspiring a universal cry of 'Vivat Rex'

82 (*Right*) Henry VIII, by Holbei
Younger: about

83 (*Far right*) Thomas Cranmer,
by Gerhardt Flicke: the archbi
holds the Pauline Ep

in London and the south-east, and it readily linked up with Lutheranism through the merchants of the London-Antwerp trade. From an Antwerp base outside the reach of English authority, Tyndale's *New Testament* and other controversial writings poured into the country during the decade after 1526. Already since about 1520 the younger Cambridge theologians had been quietly meeting in the White Horse Tavern to discuss Lutheran doctrines, and from this clerical group sprang most of the English Protestant leaders. Their usual chairman was the Augustinian friar Robert Barnes, who presently fled the realm and visited Luther at Wittenberg. The writings of Barnes closely follow Luther's arguments and Luther tenderly referred to him as 'St Robert' when he was martyred in 1540.

On his quarrel with the Spanish-controlled Papacy over his divorce, Henry VIII called to power Thomas Cromwell and Thomas Cranmer, both in their different ways near-Lutherans. Amid the enthusiasm or acquiescence of his Parliament, almost all his prelates and the great majority of his lay subjects, the King severed his

102

national Church from Rome, governed its affairs by a statutory royal supremacy, confiscated the monasteries and with them half the ecclesiastical property in England. More surprisingly, he was induced by Cromwell and Cranmer to disseminate the English Bible in translations by his exiled Protestant subjects, Tyndale and Coverdale. From this point, no European people was more profoundly influenced by the vernacular Scriptures. During the years of his power (1532–40) Cromwell openly worked for an alliance with Saxony and the other Protestant states, using Barnes himself as an intermediary. The failure of the King's marriage with Anne of Cleves—arranged under the auspices of her relative the Elector of Saxony—led at length to Cromwell's fall and execution, yet Protestantism continued its covert expansion even during the King's last reactionary years. When from 1547 they were permitted to come into the open under the regency of Protector Somerset, Zwinglian, Calvinist and other non-Lutheran influences began to gain predominance both inside and outside the nascent Anglican Church.

For social historians the ministry of Thomas Cromwell and the reign of Edward VI have inevitably been dominated by the figures of unscrupulous politicians and grasping purchasers of monastic lands. Yet simultaneously there unfolded genuine aspirations toward a more equitable if less ecclesiastical society, a practical if limited Utopia applied to a real country. This spirit is well exemplified by Cromwell's injunctions of 1536 and 1538, which sought not only to disseminate Bibles but to order the nation through better educational opportunity and vocational training. Cromwell's humanist pamphleteers Thomas Starkey and Richard Morrison did not merely thunder against rebellion; they understood that its roots lay in a society riddled with economic grievances. A decade later this critique was developing under ever more strongly Protestant influences. Its exemplars may be seen in the so-called 'Commonwealth Men', in the sermons of Hugh Latimer, in the political and literary activities of Thomas Smith and John Hales. Later still the obvious heirs of this English pragmatic tradition appear among the Puritan social idealists.

LUTHERAN LEADERSHIP IN DECLINE

By the decade 1550–60 the wonderful dynamic released by Luther's career had noticeably diminished. While the dislike of the Lutherans for the Swiss Reformers grew ever more bitter, there arose a serious internal schism between the strict Lutherans and the followers of Melanchthon, called Philippists. The latter not only modified Luther's eucharistic teaching, but even, by their doctrine of synergism, assigned to the human will a certain rôle of co-operation with the Holy Spirit in the act of conversion. This division was to weaken the Lutherans—until 1577–80, when by the Formula of Concord the great majority accepted 'strict' doctrine, including man's total depravity since the Fall. Meanwhile the repute and the political security of the Lutheran cause had for many years suffered from the unwise and ambitious conduct of its lay defenders. No one could conceal the bigamous character of the marriage contracted in 1540 by Philip of Hesse. It had been attended by Melanchthon and condoned by Luther, who inexcusably adjured Philip to keep the matter

4 Duke Maurice of Saxony,
by Cranach the Elder

quiet and 'tell a good strong lie for the sake and good of the Christian church'. More important, failures of generalship by the princes had in 1547 allowed the Emperor to subjugate their German allies, Württemberg, Ulm, Augsburg and Nuremberg. The Interim of Augsburg, now imposed upon the places in his power, was neither a genuine compromise nor intended by Charles as a permanent settlement. By remodelling town councils and expelling Protestant pastors, he hoped to win over these areas by a mixture of force and persuasion. For four years his good fortune held. The treachery practised by the young Duke Maurice of Albertine Saxony against his cousin the Elector John Frederick enabled Charles's Spanish forces under Alva to destroy the Lutheran army at Mühlberg, overrun Electoral Saxony and imprison both the Elector and Philip of Hesse. Having, however, used this period of co-operation with the Emperor to further his own unscrupulous ambitions, Duke Maurice again changed sides in 1552. In alliance with France, he compelled Charles by the Treaty of Passau to liberate his princely captives and promise freedom of worship to the Lutherans. Finally, his death in battle against the predatory Margrave of Bayreuth allowed the moderates to make peace with the Emperor. The career of Maurice had proved the impossibility of converting the Empire into a Habsburg autocracy based on Spanish pikes, and the outcome was the *cujus regio, ejus religio* principle of the Peace of Augsburg. This meant in effect that the subjects of each state must conform to its official religion, whether Catholic or Lutheran, or else emigrate.

It is customary to impugn this compromise because it failed to recognize Calvinism, yet the necessity for such recognition had not by this date become clear in the Empire. The Peace of Augsburg certainly evidenced little gift for prophecy, either in this matter or in the ambiguities of its 'ecclesiastical reservation'. The latter clause enjoined that those ecclesiastical rulers of the Empire who in future accepted conversion to Protestantism must forfeit their lands and titles. It omitted, however, to provide for a contingency soon to occasion bitter disputes: that a cathedral chapter, itself converted to Lutheranism, might proceed to elect a Lutheran bishop or administrator. Nevertheless, despite such imperfections, the Treaty of Augsburg set the tone for that long period of almost bloodless rivalry which subsisted until the outbreak of the Thirty Years War. It would indeed seem juster to place the blame for the final tragedy upon the rulers of the early seventeenth century, rather than upon those who negotiated at Augsburg in 1555. In any event, the Treaty roughly marks the end of the first phase of Protestant expansion, a triumph of resource and devotion worthy to be matched with the subsequent counterstroke of the Jesuits. During its progress Lutheranism had become closely intertwined with the rise of other Protestant movements which we must now seek to analyse.

85 Death comes to the Monk: woodcut from the Dance of Death series by Holbein the Younger, 1538

THE SWISS BACKGROUND

The forms and the destiny of Zwinglianism were deeply affected by political and social conditions peculiar to Switzerland. Yet these conditions Zwingli in his turn sought to dominate, for unlike Luther he combined the rôles of statesman and religious reformer. The Swiss cantons, having thrown off the Habsburg yoke, had freed themselves from anachronistic loyalties to Empire and Emperor. In religion and politics alike, their thought often showed itself more bracing, astringent and radical than that of other nations. They had begun to think as free men, less encumbered by history and by irrational reverences than the rest of the Germanic peoples. A mere map of their Confederation can easily deceive a man who has not seen the vastness and verticality of the Alps. Stretched like a thin web along thousands of miles of valleys, the political bonds remained somewhat fragile and subject to many tensions; the Swiss were bound together by common habits of thought, not by the centripetal force of government.

The Confederation had no capital, no head of state, no common law or coinage. The ruling classes of the three major city-states Zürich, Berne and Basle swam on the flood-tide of wealth, self-confidence, military prowess and cultured living. The threat of each of these centres to dominate the surrounding towns and districts tended to drive the latter together in self-defence. The rural cantons in general were by no means prepared to become the *contadi* of cities. At no great distance from Zürich itself, Uri, Schwyz, Unterwalden, Zug, Glarus and even Lucerne had developed little beyond the stage of peasant-farmer republics; they had been the founders of Swiss liberty and believed in the equality of free men and the sovereignty of popular assemblies. Their bitter quarrel with Zürich was to produce the last act in Zwingli's personal tragedy and set

107

permanent bounds to the triumph of the Reformation in Switzerland. Again, while the years of the Peasants' Revolt saw similar stirrings around the Lake of Constance, the Swiss farmers feared the oppression of cities rather than that of princes and feudal lords.

The winning of a relative freedom and the successful exercise of local government did not make the Swiss of the early sixteenth century a settled and contented nation. The great majority remained poor men, the victims of an unfavourable balance of trade which they strove to rectify by the soulless and degrading export of mercenary forces to Italy and other theatres of war. Their victories on behalf of the Holy League were submerged in 1515 by the disaster at Marignano, and there followed a public revulsion against the system. Even in the relatively prosperous cities there appeared the usual rifts between governing oligarchies and less privileged orders, while the craft-guilds tended on the whole to be gaining weight. In Zürich at least, the aristocratic council deigned to consult with the guilds, while the working classes showed a vital interest in public affairs. Berne, the second most powerful city, lay at the centre of great commercial routes and here the artisanry had little influence upon the mercantile patricians. Her foreign policy also differed from that of Zürich. The latter maintained close touch with the cities of south-western Germany, which were soon to become so important in Reformation politics. Geography nevertheless bade her remain mindful of the Emperor. On the other hand, Berne looked towards France; she could in large part ignore the Habsburgs and thus solve her religious problems more independently.

So far as concerns religious affairs, the complexity of the patterns and the importance of local thinking deserve the strongest emphasis. The six dioceses of Constance, Basle, Chur, Lausanne, Sion and Geneva did not territorially correspond with cantons or derive much secular support from cantonal governments. This divorce of authorities, together with slow and circuitous communications, did much to prevent effective episcopal control. Church affairs tended to remain local affairs; both cantonal and city governments had already become accustomed to a large share in their management. While on the eve of the Zwinglian Reformation biblical humanism and

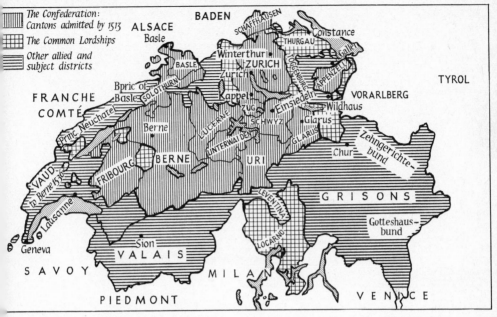

BADEN
ALSACE
Basle
SCHAFFHAUSEN
Constance
THURGAU
Winterthur
ZURICH
Zurich
TYROL
FRANCHE
COMTÉ
Bpric of
Basle
SOLOTHURN
Neuchâtel
Berne
Kappel
ZUG
Einsiedeln
Wildhaus
VORARLBERG
SCHWYZ
Glarus
TOGGENBURG
APPENZELL
ST GALLEN
Princ. Neuchâtel
LUCERNE
UNTERWALDEN
GLARUS
Chur
Zehngerichtebund
VAUD
to Berne 1536
FRIBOURG
BERNE
URI
GRISONS
Lausanne
LEVENTINA
Gotteshaus-
bund
Geneva
Sion
VALAIS
LOCARNO
SAVOY
MILAN
VENICE
PIEDMONT

86 Map of Switzerland in the sixteenth century

Erasmian criticism were affecting educated groups in the cities, it
would be untrue to say that heresy was common in Switzerland or
to deny that a solid Catholic piety flourished in the rural areas. On
the other hand, anticlericalism had become widespread; monasteries
often made exacting and unpopular landlords, while tithes were paid
under protest. An uninspired clergy, much addicted to concubinage,
commanded little intellectual and moral respect as distinct from
the reverence attached to its sacramental functions. Political antipapalism was nevertheless weaker than in many countries, the
Papacy being among the most regular employers of Swiss troops.
All in all, the Church may be thought to have inspired boredom
rather than hatred. Events were soon to reveal that the Swiss had
retained untapped sources of spirituality and a propensity for
religious enthusiasms hitherto little aroused by Catholicism.

The Zwinglian movement should not be viewed solely against a
Swiss background. Even in the early stages its doctrines came to
exercise no small influence upon the towns of south-western

87, 88 As People's Priest at the Zürich Great Minster (*left*) Zwingli preached a reform strongly backed by an independent and vigorous municipality. Zwingli's portrait by

Germany, which were not only neighbours and trading associates of the Swiss, but which by their independence of outlook and their social complexion had affinities with the Swiss towns rather than with those of central and northern Germany. We have already observed the case of the most important, the Imperial free city of Strassburg, which sought to steer her own proud course between Luther and Zwingli, and under Bucer's influence became a great centre of refuge for Protestant exiles and radicals. Unfortunately Strassburg and her neighbours lacked both the natural defences and the formidable military reputation of the Swiss, while they lay not only within the bounds of the Holy Roman Empire but within the strategic orbit of Charles V.

The geographically and theologically marginal position of these towns should warn us against pinning the textbook labels 'Lutheran', 'Zwinglian', 'Calvinist' to places, groups and individuals. While broad currents may be detected, the religious Reformation is revealed by modern research as an ocean in turmoil. Among the informed theologians there existed much eclecticism, while alongside them

Hans Asper records his death in the second Battle of Kappel, 1531, a result in part of the over-identification of his reform with the new urban and educated classes

lived many religious men in whom a little knowledge and a great deal of over-confidence bred hybrid or personal theologies. On the popular level a man might seize upon slogans from heretical sources old and new: alternatively, superstitious reflection on some emotional experience or dramatic event might cause him to invest some debatable view with a divine sanction. As we pass from Lutheranism to Zwinglianism, to Anabaptism, to Calvinism, Anglicanism and reformed Catholicism, we should grossly simplify sixteenth-century religion if we pictured it as consisting merely of these six armies marching in step under the banners of their several generals.

THE RISE OF ZWINGLI

Huldreich Zwingli probably owed more to Luther than he imagined or was willing to allow, yet he had few temperamental or intellectual traits in common with the Saxon Reformer, and he made his impact upon history from a very different angle. Certainly he affords a less interesting case-history for the psychiatrist. His youth was not beset by spiritual torments or exaggerated scruples. His approach to

111

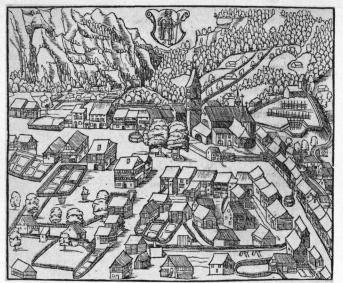

89 Glarus, the chief town of Zwingli's native canton, and his first parish: wood-cut of 1548

90 The unhappy fate of a Sw indulgence-pedlar

religion was unmystical; his very presence exuded a cheerful and manly optimism. When in 1518 he was applying for the position of People's Priest in the Great Minster at Zürich, he admitted with an engaging blend of regret and candour to a few sexual lapses, taking some consolation from the fact that he had not associated with nuns, innocent girls or married women. At Wildhaus in the Toggenburg Valley, where the family farmstead may still be seen, his father was *Amann* or elected bailiff, while his uncle Bartholomew rose from local parish priest to rural dean and rector of Weesen. The latter sent Huldreich to schools in Basle and in Berne. Matriculating in 1498 at Vienna, the young Zwingli was rusticated for some misdemeanour but afterwards readmitted. In 1502 he returned to study at the small University of Basle, where he graduated MA four years later.

A couple of decades before Luther's notoriety, Zwingli already encountered some Protestant opinions. In mature years, he expressed gratitude to one of his Basle teachers Thomas Wyttenbach, who had urged upon him that 'the traffic in indulgences was mere charlatanry and lying', and that 'the death of Christ alone was the price paid for the remission of sins'. This statement lends interest to the fact that at least three other leading Reformers, Wolfgang Capito (1478–1541),

Conrad Pellicanus and Leo Jüd, were also pupils of Thomas Wyttenbach. Even so, the overwhelming educational influence upon Zwingli was that of classical Latin literature, to which he owed at least as much as did Calvin, and from which even amid his heaviest public labours he continued to draw inspiration. From 1513 he enlarged his humanist foundations by learning Greek. By this time he was writing his earliest works: political fables warning the good Swiss against the machinations of foreign powers, yet still supporting their alliance with the pope. Naturally enough, he became a hero-worshipper of Erasmus, whom he met at Basle in 1516 and with whom he began a correspondence. Later on his friend Capito was to write: 'While Luther was in the hermitage and had not yet emerged into the light, Zwingli and I took counsel how to cast down the pope. For then our judgement was maturing under the influence of Erasmus and by reading good authors.' Zwingli's work was in effect a daring extension of the critical principles of Erasmus, applied to doctrine as well as to abuses and applied by a man more willing than Erasmus to sacrifice the amenities of a scholar's life. For the rest, Capito's statement glosses over the consistent papalism of the young Zwingli (who received a papal pension until 1520) and betrays the usual desire of the Swiss Reformers to appear wholly independent of Wittenberg. It remains true that Zwingli was working his way towards a Scriptural religion before he heard of and applauded Luther in 1518–19; he was sincere when he wrote: 'I have not learnt the teachings of Christ from Luther but from the very Word of God.'

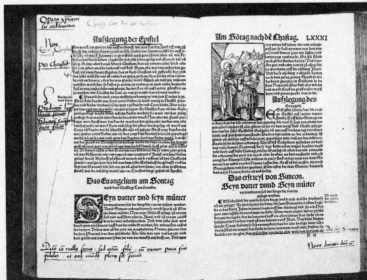

91 Zwingli owed more to the Wittenberg Reformer than he was inclined to acknowledge. His copy of Luther's exegesis of the Epistles and Gospels (Basle, Adam Petri, 1522) is full of his own marginal notes

In 1506, probably through the influence of his ever-useful uncle, Zwingli had become parish priest of Glarus and thenceforth taken part in the public affairs of that not unimportant town. As field-chaplain to his parishioners on campaign, he witnessed their victory at Novara in 1513 and their defeat at Marignano two years later. His subsequent protests against the mercenary system were based upon first-hand knowledge. In 1516, installing a vicar at Glarus, he accepted the cure of Einsiedeln, where the shrine of the Virgin formed the most famous centre of pilgrimage in Switzerland. With increasing assiduity he was now reading the New Testament, just published in the Greek text of Erasmus with its new Latin translation. He was already making contrasts between primitive and current Christianity, already in revolt against indulgences and other un-scriptural accretions, when in 1518 he went as People's Priest to the Great Minster of Zürich, prepared to use this eminent office to initiate a local Reformation.

The social patterns of the State about to play so great a rôle in Reformation history show no very dramatic features. Zürich with 7,000 inhabitants was small compared with the major German cities, but nevertheless the largest town in the Confederation and the usual meeting-place of the Diet. It also ruled a countryside with a popula-tion of some 50,000 and the towns of Winterthur and Stein am Rhein with a further 5,000. Its buoyant trade had long compensated for the decline of its weaving, and the sources afford little evidence of economic discontent or abnormally restive social groups. The city had no great banking houses: while wealthy masters tended to dominate the craft-guilds, the social structure was less oppressive than those of many other places. On the great and small councils there were some 200 seats, allowing a fairly wide participation in govern-ment. Altogether, the Zwinglian reforms cannot be said to have been based upon or accompanied by any strong urge toward social revolution. A recent analysis of some thirty-nine of Zwingli's known supporters suggests that they were led by the younger members of the oligarchy, in particular by merchants, metal-smiths and members of other trades in which economic and technical development had been marked. Of twenty-eight opposition-leaders similarly investigated,

92 Swiss mercenaries at Einsiedeln, where Zwingli was incumbent 1516–18, pass their time at national games as they wait for the Emperor's paymaster: miniature from Diebold Schilling's *Lucerne Chronicle*

no less than eleven came from the more conservative patrician families, which provided most of the mercenary officers. Some butchers and millers, whose trades suffered from Zwingli's quarrel with the agrarian Catholic cantons, also figure among the opposition. From the beginning strong support arose from among the artisans, but it appears to have waned as the Zwinglian programme failed to bring tangible concessions to this class. This growing apathy among the lower orders probably contributed towards the final military catastrophe.

The key to the changes accomplished by Zwingli lay in his preaching and that of his associates Jüd, Pellicanus and Myconius before the lay magistracy. The latter contained many apt pupils, even though its collective response was sometimes slow and hesitant. Though he met opposition from Catholics, indifferentists and men more radical than himself, Zwingli was not creating and voicing national opinion in the manner of Luther. Rather was he jockeying the council of a city where every man of note knew every other. On the door of the Great Minster we may still read that the Gospel was first preached there on 1 January 1519, but the Zürich Reformation proved in fact a rather deliberate process. Zwingli asked for the abolition of the Mass in 1523, but this was voted—and then only by a small majority—two years later. From the first the movement was more rigidly centred than that of Luther upon a search for precise biblical authority. Images, pictures and church-music soon suffered denunciation. In 1522 a company of Zürichers solemnly broke the Lenten fast by eating smoked sausages at the house of the printer Christoph Froschauer. About the same time the Bishop of Constance was petitioned to allow clerical marriage, while Zwingli himself espoused a young widow. In January 1523 a more crucial stage arrived when his sixty-seven articles were publicly debated and accepted by the city council. By the end of that year diocesan and papal authority were abrogated; by the following summer organs, relics and images were finally removed, monasteries and nunneries in full process of dissolution. Shortly afterwards the abbess of the Fraumünster, the ancient house which had once owned the city, transferred her foundation to the latter in exchange for a handsome pension. With this and other monastic endowments the city fathers then created a remarkable scheme of poor-relief and founded a theological college. Finally in 1525 they abolished the Mass in favour of Zwingli's communion-service, which sought to reproduce a simple meal of commemoration. The laity, followed by the ministers, communicated in both kinds at a table and from plain vessels. The sweeping changes also included a new order of baptism and 'prophesyings', or regular exercises in scriptural knowledge.

Zwingli now became more deeply involved in polemics concerning the Mass. His whole theology was coloured by a certain rationalism and a strong sense of the cleavage between the flesh and the spirit; in his anti-materialism he regarded the conveying of grace by material objects as a notion not merely impossible but profoundly distasteful. He became wholly convinced that Christ's words of institution at the Last Supper had been intended in a symbolic and figurative sense. He even used the old Wycliffite argument, that since Christ's body ascended into heaven, it could not be locally present in bread and wine; yet by reflecting on the Lord's death, the communicant received a spiritual blessing from this symbolic eating and drinking. Strongly divergent on the eucharist from Luther, he nevertheless accepted the latter's teaching on justification and predestination. In his optimism, he felt less keenly than Luther the deep and tragic antinomies arising from Pauline doctrine. As a true humanist and an admirer of non-Christian saints and heroes, he hoped that some means of salvation might be extended even to these:

'Hercules, Theseus, Socrates, Aristides, Antigonus, Numa, Camillus, the Catos and Scipios. . . . In a word, no good man has ever existed, nor shall there exist a holy mind, a faithful soul, from the very foundation of the world to its consummation, whom you will not see there with God.'

This generous treatment Zwingli did not, however, extend to the living Anabaptists, who were now flourishing under his shadow at Zürich, and to whom his own doubts about the authenticity of infant baptism had supplied weapons. With Zwingli's acquiescence the death-penalty was decreed against them, and in certain cases sternly enforced by the city. Zwingli exalted the authority of the pious magistrate as ecclesiastical reformer in terms more decisive than those of Luther. Whereas Luther had primarily undertaken the task of restoring a Christocentric religion, Zwingli undertook a further phase of the Reformation: the systematic imposition of Christian discipline upon the community. The theocracy composed of magistrates and pastors was the invention of Zwingli's Zürich, and it was bequeathed by them to Calvin, who consummated their experiment in Geneva. In Zürich the old Marriage Court was reconstructed as a court of morals and it exercised a general surveillance which closely foreshadowed Calvinist practice. To the Swiss Reformers, a city council with a strong lay element of cultivated Bible-students seemed indeed a more perfect instrument than the godliest of Luther's godly princes. Nevertheless, in the eyes of Zwingli's more radical supporters the movement had ended in reaction and anticlimax. Arising in an atmosphere of Christian liberty and congregational autonomy, it had swiftly hardened into a State Church. In his treatise *Of Divine and Human Justice* (1523) Zwingli accepted this as inevitable. Moreover, he now rejected the notion that any ideal society could be shaped within this sinful world and he was careful to explain that existing contractual obligations must continue to be honoured. Therefore, whatever might have been said against tithes during the first careless rapture, they must still be paid. Like Luther he had been compelled to reconcile his social idealism with his need for the support of existing governments. And from the first these governments were guiltless of any hasty designs to attain the earthly paradise.

The completion of the Zürich experiment took place alongside a fairly rapid expansion of the Reformed religion. Zwingli's converts were preaching in a number of towns during the years 1521-3, when Schaffhausen, St Gallen and Appenzell adopted the new doctrines. By this time also Glarus and Zwingli's native district of Toggenburg had been largely won, though in all the rural areas there remained a substantial body of Catholic dissent. Farther afield, the Grisons and the other allies of the south-east entertained an old feud with the bishops of Chur and also felt suspicious of Austria, Milan and Venice.

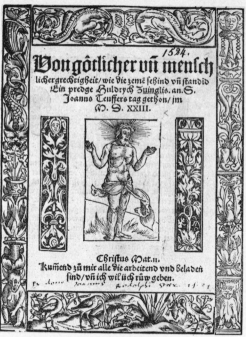

93 Johannes Hussgen (Oecolampadius) of Basle: portrait from Theodore Beza's *Icones*, 1580

94 The new burghers' church in Zürich found reassurance in Zwingli's *Of Divine and Human Justice*

These secular emotions worked in favour of the travelling Zwinglian preachers, who rode or trudged the long valleys with their packs of printed literature. By 1526 their cause had become strong in such outlying areas, though it never made an outright conquest. More crucial to its national success were the attitudes of Berne and Basle. Since 1520 Pellicanus, Capito and others had been active in Basle, which, although a centre of humanism and the home of Erasmus, was also the see of a resident bishop and lay uncomfortably close to Habsburg territories. In November 1522 John Hussgen, *alias* Oecolampadius, arrived in Basle. Hitherto known as a Hebraist and a helper of Erasmus in his biblical studies, this cleric now displayed a remarkable gift for practical affairs. He took the lead in converting the artisanry, bringing about the withdrawal of the bishop and procuring a council order which allowed the citizens freedom to absent themselves from the Mass. It was not, however, until February 1529 that the council, under heavy pressure from the guilds and the lower orders, gave exclusive recognition to the Reformed religion.

119

In some respects the initial situation at Berne seemed even less promising. This city lacked strong anticlerical traditions arising from any oppressive bishop or religious house. It stood at the head of a large rural canton, while its aristocratic government was not very responsive to pressure from below. In 1520 Zwingli's follower Berchtold Haller became a canon of the collegiate church and won much support by his preaching. Support of a less respectable kind arose from an unusually large output of popular and sometimes scurrilous pamphlets. At first the city council permitted Protestant preaching, but banned the mention of the explosive name of Luther. When the Bishop of Lausanne tried to silence Haller, the city refused to receive his mandate. In January 1528 a public debate was organized, but the Catholic bishops refused to participate, while the Reformers sent their heaviest guns: Zwingli from Zürich, Bucer from Strassburg and Oecolampadius from Basle. The result was inevitable, and in the weeks which followed Berne hastened to overtake Zürich by cancelling the authority of the bishop, dissolving the monasteries and renouncing images, crucifixes and church-music. When the conservative peasantry of the Oberland rioted against the abolition of the Mass, the city imposed the new worship upon them also. Though less distinguished by educational and charitable works, the Bernese Reformation has in retrospect an importance almost as great as that of Zürich. Protestant Berne allied with France against the ambitious Charles of Savoy, now an adherent of the Habsburgs. It then extended its influence into Vaud, and so, with western Switzerland turning towards the Reformation, the stage was prepared for Guillaume Farel's conversion of Geneva. In default of this immensely important episode at Berne, Calvin would not have been summoned to Geneva and Geneva could scarcely have maintained its independence, much less become the metropolis of the Reformed religion. Indirectly therefore, the conversion of Berne became a vital factor in the political salvation of Protestantism throughout Europe.

ZWINGLIANISM IN CONFLICT

These striking successes left untouched the Catholic cantons of Zug, Uri, Unterwalden, Lucerne and Schwyz, which continued stubbornly burning Protestants and vetoing Zwingli's proposal that toleration should be allowed in the Common Lordships (such as Thurgau), which were ruled jointly by the whole Confederation. In April 1529 the Catholics even went over to the old enemy by concluding a Christian Union with Ferdinand of Austria. When, however, Zwingli led a force against them he was constrained to make peace at Kappel through the insistence of his colleagues and the refusal of Berne to give him support. Even so, he gained some advantage, since the Catholics agreed to abandon the Austrian alliance and to allow religious freedom in the Common Lordships. Meanwhile, aware of the importance of the wavering Swiss in the politico-religious balance of power, the Lutheran military leader Philip of Hesse busily sought to reconcile Luther and Zwingli. Yet the former, long exasperated by the wiles of radical competition, obstinately regarded the Zwinglians as sectaries little less pernicious than Carlstadt and Müntzer. In the autumn Philip managed to bring the leaders together at Marburg, where two years earlier he had founded the university, the first in Europe to be started under Protestant auspices. The two parties of divines naturally found themselves able to agree upon communion for the laity in both kinds and in rejecting concepts of the Mass as a sacrifice or a 'good work'. Yet on the nature of the rite both parties had already spoken with a dogmatism beyond the conciliatory powers of Martin Bucer, who came to Marburg supposing that Luther believed not in a localized, but in a spiritual presence. At the first formal session Luther dispelled this illusion by chalking on the table the words *Hoc est corpus meum*; and with stubborn resolution he refused to entertain any doctrine of a merely symbolic or spiritual presence. On their parting with this major problem unsettled, Zwingli protested in tears his desire for friendship with the Lutherans, while Oecolampadius exclaimed: 'I beg you for the Lord's sake, give heed to the poor church.' Their anxiety and disappointment can well be imagined, since their theological failure had destroyed the chances of an alliance of immense value amid the perils which still beset the Swiss Reformation. Tenaciously but to no avail, Bucer continued to draft formulae for union, notably the *Tetrapolitana*, purporting to come from the four cities of Strassburg, Constance, Lindau and Memmingen. Yet as for Luther, he was soon to hear of Zwingli's death with more relief than sorrow.

Returning from Marburg, the Swiss Reformer arranged alliances with Strassburg, with Basle, with Philip of Hesse. Meanwhile his Catholic opponents kept touch with the Habsburgs and the hollowness of the Peace of Kappel remained apparent. Early in 1531 the Grisons, attacked by a petty Italian adventurer, appealed for aid to the Confederation: it was given by Zürich but refused by the Catholic cantons. This demonstration of disunity was followed by further disputes over religious freedom. At the end of his patience, Zwingli conceived a bold plan to subjugate and convert the Catholics. While Zürich would undertake this task, Berne would be allowed a parallel ascendancy over western Switzerland. He began by attempting to stage an economic blockade of the Catholics, but he could not stop their supplies of grain and other provisions coming up from the south. In October 1531 they declared war unexpectedly upon Zürich and found the city both politically and militarily unprepared. Left to themselves, the Swiss had the peculiar habit of fighting without generals, and the fate of Zwingli was settled by military incompetence as well as by excessive faith in divine intervention and by sheer inferiority in numbers. Meeting 8,000 Catholics at Kappel with a hastily gathered force of only 2,500, Zwingli died in action, personally bearing arms. The end of a Christian warrior did not ill befit his life.

With him there perished not merely the hegemony of Zürich within the Confederation, but also his greater concept of a united Switzerland allied with Venice and with all the German Protestants against Habsburg-led Catholicism throughout Europe. Zwingli had stood at the head of that tradition which led on to William the Silent, to Gustavus Adolphus, to Oliver Cromwell, but all these three statesmen were to command greater forces and adopt more realistic approaches to military and material problems. Despite his initial shrewdness, Zwingli had wanted to make the Swiss Confederation sustain a more dramatic rôle in Europe than its internal development would allow. By doctrinal dogmatism he had marred the prospects for his European Protestant League. And in the last resort he perished through attempting the career of an armed prophet without maintaining a reasonable level of armament.

While the political state of Switzerland contributed so much to the ruin of Zwingli, it nevertheless contained certain guarantees that the fruits of his religious labours would not be lost. This turmoil of local interests was hard to direct, yet it also stood proof against counter-revolution. To the rout at Kappel there followed anti-climax and stalemate. The defeated Zwinglians could still assemble strong forces, but they made no serious effort at a counterstroke. On the other hand there occurred no large-scale reversion to Catholicism and the peace-treaty anticipated by a quarter of a century the formula made famous by the Peace of Augsburg: *cujus regio, ejus religio.* Each canton decided its own religion, except that in the Common Lord-ships the Catholic minorities were to be protected. Protestant preaching in the Catholic cantons was forbidden. While in fact a few wavering areas like Solothurn and Glarus now returned to the Catholic fold, Bernese Protestantism soon completed that vital west-ward expansion to which we have already alluded. And though Oecolampadius the attractive and scholarly leader at Basle died within a few weeks of Zwingli, direction passed into the capable hands of Heinrich Bullinger, who had just migrated to Zürich as a result of the return of Bremgarten to Catholicism.

95 Heinrich Bullinger, Zwingli's successor at the Zürich Great Minster: anonymous painted portrait

Still in his twenties, Bullinger succeeded Zwingli as chief pastor of Zürich and worked indefatigably until his death in 1575. He had the intelligence never to repeat the Bible-and-sword methods of his predecessor, but like Erasmus and Calvin he became an epistolary crusader, maintaining a most influential correspondence with Protestant rulers and leaders all over Europe. With the passage of years Bullinger came to be revered and consulted as an oracle second only to Calvin. He educated many of the English Protestants and welcomed at Zürich the fugitives from Mary Tudor's persecution. In his last years his authority supported Queen Elizabeth against Puritan extremism; he also helped to prepare her reply to the papal excommunication. Yet Bullinger's greatest achievement lay in his statesmanship at home. While his First Helvetic Confession of 1536 still contained some Lutheran elements, in that same year Calvin burst upon the scene and during the succeeding decade pointed the need for a very different orientation. By the Zürich Agreement (*Consensus Tigurinus*) of 1549 on the Lord's Supper and by the Second Helvetic Confession of 1566, Bullinger united the forces of Zwinglianism and Calvinism into one Reformed religion, a faith able to conquer lands which Zwingli never knew.

96 Zwingli's signature is the second on the Swiss copy of the Marburg Protocol of 1529. The others are: Oecolampadius of Basle; Martin Bucer and Caspar Hedio of Strassburg; Luther, Justus Jonas and Melanchthon; Andreas Osiander of Nuremburg, Stephen Agricola of Augsburg, and Johann Brenz of Schwäbisch Hall. In the German copy (at Marburg) the Wittenberg delegation signed first

THE RISE OF ANABAPTISM

Like so many revolutionary movements, the Protestant Reformation swiftly gave birth to enthusiasts who sought to outbid and displace its original leaders. We have already observed how Carlstadt and Müntzer attempted to redirect the great volume of popular protest brought to a head by the career of Luther. The movement headed by Zwingli was even more prone to attract first the support and later the rivalry of men to whom it seemed not radical enough. Zwingli had indeed ruthlessly simplified worship, rationalized eucharistic doctrine and debated the Scriptural validity of infant baptism. The first groups called Anabaptists, headed by Conrad Grebel, Balthasar Hübmaier and Felix Mantz came from among his Zürich disciples and claimed to be carrying his thought to logical conclusions. Like Luther, Zwingli indignantly refused to travel with such men; he fully endorsed the savage tactics used against them by the magistrates of Zürich and other Swiss cities. The alacrity with which he accepted the rule of the godly magistrate was prompted almost as much by the need to contain radicalism as by the need to dislodge Catholicism.

Anabaptism had connections with medieval heresy and prophecy; even the organized movements did not spring solely from Zürich. They can also be traced back to the chaotic Wittenberg of 1521, when infant baptism was being questioned, and when the Zwickau prophets attempted to erect a separatist church. It was from this Lutheran background that Müntzer emerged and made his bid to deflect the peasant rebels towards religious extremism. Müntzer was active in various places later notable as Anabaptist centres, and despite the attempts of modern Mennonites to eject him from the ranks of their founding fathers, it seems certain that he exercised real influence upon certain Anabaptists. One of his liveliest followers,

97 Hans Huth: portrait by Christoffel van Sichem, from his *Iconica* (Arnhem, 1609)

Hans Huth, later became an acknowledged Anabaptist leader. In general, however, it has been held that the chief source of the Anabaptist river was the Zürich of 1523–5, where Grebel and Mantz, possibly inspired by contacts with both Müntzer and Carlstadt, argued the question of infant baptism with Zwingli and encouraged the citizens to refuse the rite for their children. Early in 1525 they actually began baptizing upon profession of faith, Grebel christening the priest Georg Blaurock, who in turn christened fifteen other adults. Decisively rejecting Zwingli's leadership, the group soon afterwards held simplified communion-services of a commemorative character and behaved as a 'gathered church' or autonomous sect. In Zürich, the first movement took place not among the city-dwellers but among the peasants and rural artisans of the extra-mural territory. Within a few weeks large numbers were baptized in the small towns and villages, some of them by immersion in rivers. Educated leaders had touched off genuinely popular emotions, while subsequently the rejection of conservative Protestantism may have been strengthened by Luther's denunciation of the German peasants. Later in the year, the Zürich authorities not only imprisoned Grebel, Mantz and Blaurock but subjected Hübmaier to torture, recantation and banishment. In March 1526 they enacted that Anabaptists should be drowned 'without mercy' and the following January executed this sentence against Mantz. Grebel

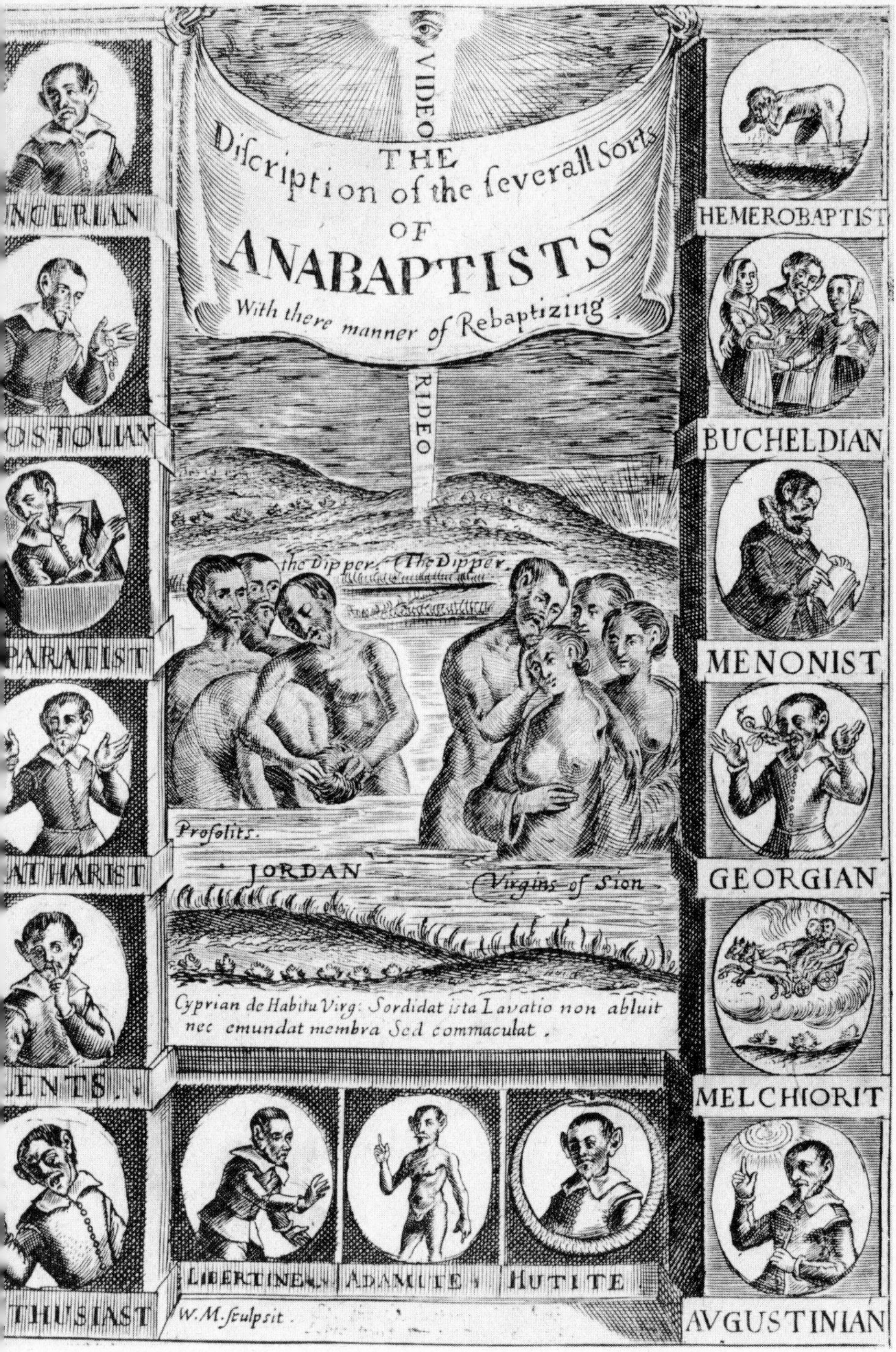
VIDEO
THE
Discription of the severall Sorts
OF
ANABAPTISTS
With there manner of Rebaptizing.
RIDEO
the Dipper
The Dipper
Prosolits.
JORDAN
Virgins of Sion
Cyprian de Habitu Virg: Sordidat ista Lavatio non abluit nec emundat membra Sed commaculat.
NCERIAN
OSTOLIAN
PARATIST
ATHARIST
ENTS
THUSIAST
HEMEROBAPTIST
BUCHELDIAN
MENONIST
GEORGIAN
MELCHIORIT
AVGUSTINIAN
LIBERTINES
ADAMITES
HUTITE
W.M. sculpsit

98 The proliferation of Anabaptist sects became at last a subject for ridicule: title-page of Daniel Featley's Description of 1645, known also as 'The Dippers Dipt'

had meanwhile escaped by natural death, while Blaurock as a non-citizen was beaten through the streets and expelled. From this stage the sect lingered in remoter places, but its main expansion occurred outside Switzerland.

During the later 'twenties and the 'thirties Anabaptism spread wildly amongst poor townsmen and peasants in many European countries. One of its typical figures is Hans Huth, a wandering book-binder and bookseller with a following in scores of villages and towns throughout south Germany and Austria. His main base in later years was Augsburg, but he appeared as far afield as Nikolsburg in Moravia, where his apocalyptic prophecies aroused opposition from the exiled Hübmaier. In 1527 Huth was arrested in Augsburg and interrogated under torture; later in the year he died as a result of burns, sustained by accident or in an attempt to escape. Not un-deservedly, he filled the rôle of a Pied Piper in the German folk-legend of a later day. Meanwhile Anabaptism scored one of its greatest successes in Moravia, where Hübmaier found ready listeners and readers of his pamphlets among the German population, the Hussites and the recent converts to Lutheranism. As a former cathedral preacher of Regensburg, he had a far better professional training than the common run of sectarian missionaries and his efforts were reinforced by the exiled Zürich printer Froschauer. By the time they were disturbed by the apocalyptic and millenarian preaching of Huth, they had already won over the baronial house of Lichtenstein, certain Lutheran pastors and some thousands of the laity. When the Lichtensteins had imprisoned Huth (who had rejected the State and refused to pay war-taxation) Hübmaier had approved their action, citing Scripture to defend the authority of the civil power. Nevertheless in 1528 even the sober Hübmaier suffered arrest and condemnation by the Imperial government. He and his loyal wife were sent to Vienna, he to be burned at the stake, she to be cast into the Danube with a great stone around her neck.

Moving to the neighbourhood of Austerlitz, others of the Moravian Anabaptists received powerful reinforcement from that remarkable organizer Jakob Hutter (d. 1536) and a large body of his Tyrolese followers. In the few years before his own burning at

99, 100 The mild, biblical communalism of the Hutterites, seen (*left*) on the title-page of an Anabaptist apologia of 1589, drew the ridicule of many, as (*right*) the Ingolstadt author of *The Hutterite Anabaptist Dove-cote* of 1607 (from the title-page)

Innsbrück, he established over eighty Anabaptist settlements in Moravia. These often held goods in community, but so far from encouraging social extravagances, Hutter shaped them into earnest and hard-working communities. Undergoing a further spell of persecution during the middle decades of the century, driven from one area to another, they not only survived but created an astonishing network of friends and converts in central Europe, in Poland and in Italy. For many years they continued to derive support and recruits from the Tyrolese communities which had been founded by Blaurock between his exile from Zürich and his execution three years later. Some of the Moravian groups went on to participate in the colonization of America, their successors in the United States being still known as Hutterites or Hutterian Brethren.

For several years the city of Strassburg under the liberal inspiration of Wolfgang Capito and Martin Bucer granted hospitality to a host of Anabaptists, quite apart from other assorted radicals like Carlstadt, Denck, Schwenckfeld and Servetus. When in 1534 Strassburg accepted the Confession of Augsburg, which condemned Anabaptist doctrines, there were said to be 2,000 Anabaptists in a population not much more than ten times their number. Amongst these had lived until recently the former Tyrolese mining-engineer Pilgram Marbéck, who had at first attained respect in Strassburg, but had been banished in 1532 and thenceforth enjoyed great success in

129

organizing Anabaptist communities throughout southern Germany. This Tyrolese mining background incidentally serves to stress the importance of local factors. Swiftly developing through Fugger investment, its large, understaffed parishes flooded by immigrant workers, it proved a classic focus of Anabaptism.

THE MELCHIORITES AND MÜNSTER

The evil genius of Anabaptism was Melchior Hoffmann (c. 1500–1543). Originally a leather-dresser from Waldshut, this man had quarrelled with Zwingli, visited Wittenberg, and worked both as a Lutheran missionary and a fur-trader in Livonia. By 1529 he was engaging Bugenhagen in disputation at Flensburg, denying consubstantiation and dismissing Luther as the mere herald of the true Reformation. Banished from Denmark, he joined the Anabaptists in Strassburg and submitted to rebaptism. Between 1530 and 1533 Hoffmann performed his most important rôle in religious history by laying the foundations of the movement in Holland and East Friesland. At the end of this period he announced that Strassburg had been chosen as the New Jerusalem, from which the 144,000 heralds mentioned in *Revelation* xiv, 1 would go forth to spread Anabaptism over the whole world. By now, however, the Strassburg leaders Bucer and Capito were leading the city authorities against

101, 102 Bernhard Knipperdolling, the richest of the twelve elders of John of Leyden's new kingdom, engraved by Heinrich Aldegrever in 1536; and Melchior Hoffmann, a portrait by van Sichem from *Het Tooneel der Hoofketteren*, edition of 1677

Anabaptism, and the prophet Melchior spent the last decade of his life in prison. An imaginative fanatic, convinced that divine inspiration dispensed with the need for learning, Hoffmann entertained a number of hitherto unusual doctrines which passed into widespread currency. Echoing an ancient Gnostic teaching, though in all likelihood unconsciously, he insisted that Jesus did not actually take flesh from his Mother, that his nature was single and wholly divine, without a link to the sinful Adam.

There were no doubt even wilder sectaries than Melchior Hoffmann, yet it was his wing of the movement which ran amok and brought general disaster. The Netherlands leadership was assumed by his disciple the Haarlem baker Jan Matthys, while from 1530 conversions multiplied in Amsterdam, Leyden, Deventer, Zwolle and Kampen. In 1533–4 the Dutch Anabaptists learned that in the episcopal city of Münster religious radicals were not only defying the Catholic Prince Bishop but ousting the Lutherans from influence. Accordingly the Dutchmen organized a mass-emigration to Münster, only to find themselves turned back by the Netherlands authorities and subjected to fierce persecution. Meanwhile Münster itself slid toward thoroughgoing Anabaptism, led by the popular preacher and ex-Lutheran Bernhard Rothmann, who denounced infant baptism and advocated a community of goods. Supported by

103, 104 Michael Servetus (*left*) and Jan Matthys of Haarlem: from *Het Tooneel der Hoofketteren* (1677), a 'gallery' of modern prophets. Servetus' execution at the order of Calvin, and Matthys' death in a sortie from the besieged city of Munster, are seen in the background

105 John of Leyden: drawing by Heinrich Aldegrever

106 (*Above*) The siege of the Anabaptist stronghold of Münster (Westphalia), 1534–5: wood-cut by Erhard Schoen

107 Various methods of interrogation included the iron horse, the rack, and stretching with weights: wood-cut by Hans Weiditz from Petrarch's *Trostspiegel* (Augsburg, 1532)

the wealthy cloth-merchant Bernhard Knipperdolling and by the lower orders, the radical group had by January 1534 gained control of the city. They were joined by many Hollanders including Jan Matthys in person, who insisted upon universal baptism and declared real property to be common. Matthys did not, however, begin to establish practical communism until the military needs of the besieged city made it expedient.

Catholics and Lutherans fled the city and by the end of February the Prince Bishop began to construct his siege-works. In April Matthys was killed leading a sortie, apparently in the belief that divine favour would enable him to conquer an army at the head of a handful of men. Command then fell into the hands of the one-time tailor John of Leyden (Jan Beukels), who dissolved the city council and established a strict theocracy under twelve elders or judges of the tribes of Israel. Sins made punishable by death included blasphemy, reviling parents, disobeying a master, adultery, spreading scandal and complaining. It is, however, just to see this code as one of military law. The introduction of polygamy also owed something to emergency conditions, since there now remained only 1,700 men in the city, but four times as many women and thousands of children to be protected. Needless to add, polygamy was defended with a great wealth of biblical texts by the ex-priest Rothmann, who went on to introduce more empirical arguments. Since the purpose of marriage was to be fruitful, a husband should not be impeded by the sterility or indisposition of one wife. Moreover women, 'who everywhere have been getting the upper hand', would no longer be able to lead men about like bears on ropes if a man was not sexually dependent upon one woman. John of Leyden, who never lacked conviction, took no less than sixteen wives, including the beautiful widow of his friend Matthys. He later beheaded one of them for impertinence, trampling on her body in the presence of the rest of the harem. Though he showed military skill, John appears to have become insane during these last stages of the siege. In the September he caused himself to be crowned king and appeared in royal regalia before bowing subjects in the market-place.

Amid great suffering and desperate efforts to procure help from outside sympathizers, the siege dragged on until 25 June 1535, when after a final assault most of the defenders were butchered by the victors. Condemned by a more leisurely process, King John, Knipperdolling and another leader were publicly tortured to death by red-hot tongs and their bodies suspended in an iron cage from the tower of St Lambert's. Everywhere the moderates, both Catholic and Protestant, took due warning from these events. 'God opened the eyes of the governments by the revolt at Münster', wrote Bullinger, 'and thereafter no one would trust even those Anabaptists who claimed to be innocent.' Persecution spread rapidly but the vast total of martyrdoms once claimed has lately been consigned by research to the realm of fantasy. A recent estimate for the whole period 1523–66 suggests two to three thousand victims in the Netherlands, not all of them Anabaptists. Even if this revision be realistic, it may still be claimed that, in relation to numbers, no religious body has displayed a greater passive heroism in the face of persecution.

108 The seven articles of the Brotherly Union of the True Children of God: the title-page of the Schleitheim Confession, an Anabaptist credo of 1527, reflects its surreptitious production

CHARACTERISTICS OF ANABAPTISM

In what sense can Anabaptism be called a 'movement'? Certainly one cannot speak of an Anabaptist Reformation as one speaks of a Lutheran, Zwinglian or Calvinist Reformation. The Anabaptists had no great spiritual leader, no generally-accepted epitome of doctrine, no central directive organs. They did not guide governments, shape national societies or control for any considerable period a functioning polity. To this withdrawn community of saints, discipleship was far from limited to believers' baptism, however essential this might appear in order to partake in redemption by Christ. One of their most widely circulated documents was the Schleitheim Confession drawn up in 1527, probably by the martyr Michael Sattler, one of the more systematic devotees driven out from Zürich. This code consists of seven articles. Baptism shall only be accorded to 'those who have learned repentance and amendment of life . . . and who walk in the resurrection of Jesus Christ'. Those in error may only be excommunicated after three warnings, and this must be done before the breaking of bread, so that only a pure and united Church will sit down together. The Lord's Supper is only for the baptized and is a memorial-service. Members must relinquish both popish and anti-popish worship, and take no part in public affairs. They must renounce warfare and 'the unchristian, devilish weapons of force'.

Pastors must be supported by congregations in order to read the Scriptures, discipline the Church and lead in prayer. If a pastor be banished or martyred, another must immediately be ordained, 'so that God's little flock and people may not be destroyed'. The sword is ordained to be used by the worldly magistrates to punish the wicked, but it must not be used even in self-defence by Christians, who should neither go to law nor serve as magistrates. In accordance with *Matthew* 34 and *James* 12, oaths are forbidden.

Altogether, it can at least be said that this Schleitheim Confession contains many characteristic positions and that most Anabaptists would broadly have accepted it. Yet outside it there were few orthodox religious or social teachings which one Anabaptist or another did not challenge. Many doctrines absent from the Schleitheim Confession were prominently maintained by some congregations, such as the Melchiorite Christology already mentioned. A general belief in free will, as opposed to the Protestant orthodoxy of predestination, marked Anabaptist thought, and it frequently suffered criticism as a revival of the Pelagian heresy. The doctrine of psychopannychism, the sleep of the soul between death and resurrection, often appeared in Anabaptist teaching, but it also occurred amongst other denominations and attracted Luther himself. Few Anabaptists taught polygamy, and while sexual innovations or orgies took place in some sectarian groups, these groups were at most on the fringes of Anabaptism. The latter did not systematically teach communism, though versions of it proved useful under pioneering conditions like those in Moravia. The most broadly subversive doctrine lay in a rejection of secular law and military duties; some Anabaptists did not merely dissociate Church and State but claimed to be an elect body justified in renouncing all obligations towards the rest of society.

During recent years we have attained a new respect for the strain of Christian idealism to be found among the Anabaptists. The mass cruelties practised against them by Protestants and Catholics alike shocks even those of us inured to the values of the sixteenth century. Despite the frenzy of Münster, despite a few advocates of violence in other places, the great majority of these sectarians were sincere and pacific, people who could have been controlled without fire and drowning. On the other side, it might be maintained that modern denominational enthusiasts tend to overestimate their positive achievement. Communities of 'saints' which abandon the rest of mankind must always be subject to close limitations. We beg many questions if we point to their spiritual descendants, the sects of seventeenth-century England and New England, and then blandly claim that the Anabaptists made immense contributions to modern religious and civic freedom. These blessings had, after all, very complex origins. There are, it is true, many fine passages in Anabaptist writings denouncing the use of the secular arm to constrain human conscience. Such passages are nevertheless to be matched in a good many other Protestant liberals, and even in a few Catholic writers of the sixteenth century. The sectarians of that age had in fact by no means that near-monopoly of tolerationist sentiment attributed to them by some of their less cautious admirers. Moreover, their practical tolerance, as one would expect, fell far short of modern liberal norms. A sect which withdraws itself from the rest of society, expels its own deviationists and restricts salvation to its own little flock can hardly claim the ancestry of Milton, of Locke, of the eighteenth-century liberators. Finally, however admirable their intentions, the Anabaptists did in effect strike a terrible blow against the more tolerant elements in Reformation thought. More decisively than the excesses of the peasant rebels, Anabaptist indiscretion blasted the infant shoots of liberalism which grew upon Lutheran and Zwinglian trees. In the imaginations of many otherwise gentle and moderate men, Anabaptism seemed no mere inchoate trend, no mere confused and wrangling congregationalism, but a vast international conspiracy to tear down the fragile social structure of Europe. In that setting, some degree of persecution hence became quite inevitable and it was by no means wholly religious in character.

MENNO SIMONS AND THE RECOVERY

Despite the disastrous exploits of Netherlanders at Münster, it was also from the Low Countries that more moderate and sensible forces emerged to save Anabaptism. By far the greatest of its new leaders

109 Menno Simons, from van Sichem, *Het Tooneel der Hoofketteren:* the Testament is open at Menno's motto, I Cor. 3:11—'For other foundation can no man lay than that is laid, which is Jesus Christ.'

was Menno Simons (1496–1561), a priest of Witmarsum in Dutch Friesland who had been baptized into the sect in 1536. Throughout the dark years between that date and his death in 1561, this intrepid organizer travelled indefatigably throughout Germany and the Netherlands, confirming and enlarging the groups which managed to survive the persecution. Though Simons received ideas from Hoffmann and Schwenckfeld, he impressed his own clear-headed character on the movement, renouncing violent tactics and ceaselessly preaching the pacific and non-resisting principles which should never have been abandoned. It was largely through his communities, later called Mennonite, that the finest traditions of Anabaptism were carried through to the seventeenth century and so enabled to make their contribution to the religious history of modern Europe and America. For example, the chief founder of the modern Baptist Church, the separatist John Smyth (d. 1612), came under Mennonite influence while in exile at Amsterdam.

Not all the Netherlandish contemporaries of Menno Simons accepted his leadership. The glass-painter David Joris (d. 1556), became another wandering organizer, a flamboyant prophet full of visions and strange experiences. He was finally compelled to flee to Basle, where living incognito for many years he managed to avoid burning—at all events until exhumed for this purpose some two years after his death. Other Anabaptists founded more esoteric movements diverging from the Mennonite mainstream. The tendency to progress into Unitarianism appeared not only in Italy but in the ex-priest Adam Pastor, who left the Mennonites in 1547 and founded an Anti-Trinitarian group lasting for several generations in the region between Cologne and Münster. The fissiparous tendency is again illustrated by Henry Niclaes (c. 1502–80), who thought himself the prophet of a wholly new age of Christianity and founded the Family of Love. Niclaes travelled widely from his base at Emden and visited England; there his sect continued to attract adherents when other forms of English Anabaptism had almost died out. Its pantheist and antinomian tendencies caused great scandal in Elizabethan times, and in 1580 it was banned by a stern proclamation. Nevertheless, the books of Niclaes were still being reprinted during the Cromwellian Protectorate and the sect survived to merge with the Quakers and other Nonconformists towards 1700.

110 An early Anabaptist execution in the Netherlands, 1524: from a Dutch martyrology of 1685

In general, English Anabaptism forms a pendent to the story of the Netherlandish movement. By 1530 several radical tracts had reached England, seemingly from Antwerp, and within two or three years there existed Anabaptist groups among the numerous Netherlandish immigrants. In 1535 fourteen of these people suffered burning in London and other places, while further victims appear later in the reign of Henry VIII. In the more liberal days of Edward VI, when continental refugees of all types crowded into England, the sect began to make native converts in London and Kent. In 1548–9 Henry Hart, leader of the Kentish group, actually printed two cautious devotional tracts, while another English Anabaptist composed a remarkable plea for religious toleration, which we know in some detail from a point-by-point reply made by John Knox. Anti-Anabaptist books were published by Bishop Hooper, by William Turner, dean of Wells, and by other eminent English ecclesiastics. The alarm of the Anglican establishment can also be gauged by the large number of the Forty-Two Articles which were devoted to the condemnation of Anabaptist doctrines. Though from this point the sect made little progress in England, as late as 1575 two Dutch Anabaptists were burned in London, and 'died in great horror, roaring and crying'. These men are also said to have denied the doctrine of the Trinity.

Around the years 1535–40 Anabaptist and Anti-Trinitarian groups formed in various Italian cities, especially in cosmopolitan Venice, where an Anabaptist conference discussed doctrines of the Trinity in the year 1550, the delegates having come chiefly from the Venetian territories, Vicenza, Padua, Treviso, and from the neighbouring Grisons. By now the Anti-Trinitarian offshoot had arisen from the twin roots of Anabaptist biblicism and Italian rationalism. Its earliest literary exponent had been Reuchlin's pupil Martin Cellarius, a former Anabaptist befriended by Capito at Strassburg, where in 1527 his little book *De Operibus Dei* set forth distinctly heterodox views on the Trinity. Only four years later the brilliant but unstable Spaniard Michael Servetus published a first Anti-Trinitarian tractate, but his developed theology appears only in his *Christianismi Restitutio* of 1553, the year of his sensational escape from the Catholic authorities of Vienne (where he had practised medicine for years under a pseudonym) and his burning by the Calvinists at Geneva. Servetus never became a thoroughgoing Unitarian, but his denial of the accepted doctrine of the Trinity and of the essential divinity of Christ forms a clear landmark in the prehistory of the sect. Meanwhile heterodox speculations regarding the Trinity had appeared in the circle of Juan Valdés, and at a later time (1563) Bernardino Ochino himself was to be expelled from his pastorate at Zürich for similar heresies. From this time the most effective Anti-Trinitarian leaders were the Sozzini, uncle and nephew, who were both intimate with Anabaptists and who brought the name Socinian to this school of thought. From Italy it spread to eastern Europe. The Piedmontese physician Giorgio Biandrata created active groups of Unitarians in Poland (1558) and in Hungary (1563). In the former Fausto Sozzini assumed the leadership, and the magnate Jan Sieninski founded the famous settlement of Rakow, whence the classic Rakovian Confession was issued in 1605. It was followed by prolonged struggles with the Jesuits, who in 1638 procured the suppression of the Unitarian college at Rakow. The final ban on the sect came twenty years later. Meanwhile in Hungary, Biandrata's group converted King John Sigismund himself, and though after his death in 1570 they underwent a period of persecution, they gained recognition as a lawful denomination in 1638. In England the rise of Unitarianism had only indirect links with these developments and the modern Church is usually regarded as springing from the tracts and conventicles of John Biddle during the period of the Commonwealth. Even so, that powerful movement which attained importance in eighteenth-century Massachusetts—and still has its chief centre in the Harvard Divinity School—takes pride in tracing its ancestry back to the first half of the sixteenth century.

SPIRITUALIST RELIGION

The distinction between Anabaptists and Spiritualists, now so widely accepted, was postulated by Ernst Troeltsch over half a century ago. At all periods, he claimed, three types of Christianity have tended to emerge. The church-type, whether Catholic or Protestant, works through the ministry, the Word and the sacraments; it is objective in its approach and attempts to supply the spiritual needs of the masses as well as those of the religiously gifted. It is hence forced into some considerable degree of compromise with the State, with secular law, perhaps even with warfare, tyranny and the abuse of private property. The Catholic Church, it is contended, effected such necessary compromises and permitted two widely differing standards, as between the secular-minded masses and the ascetic monasticism of its *élite*. Ecclesiastical Protestantism likewise compromised, yet with its doctrine of the priesthood of all believers, it sought to abolish this Catholic dualism and at least to urge its highest standard upon all men.

The second species envisaged by Troeltsch is the sect-type, so admirably exemplified in the sixteenth century by the Anabaptists. This type stresses Christ's rôle as lawgiver, and tries precisely to follow his recorded commands by forming voluntary groups of saints, withdrawn from the rest of society, claiming absolute standards and excluding the masses, who remain incapable of such standards. The sects usually founded quiet, biblicist congregations, consoling themselves with the prospect of the coming Kingdom, but occasionally using violence against the ungodly in order to hasten its arrival.

In the third place, Troeltsch recognized the Spiritualist or mystical tradition, the 'Everlasting Gospel' to which we have already alluded. This type recognizes Christ by inward experience; in its subjectivity it feels little interest in ecclesiastical organization or in ceremonies. Even a true understanding of the Bible depends upon the ability of the individual to develop this subjective understanding. Freer and more tolerant than the Anabaptist sectarians, these Spiritualists could likewise develop antinomian tendencies, but they also spoke only to an *élite*, their doctrine being incapable of permeating the masses.

As we traverse the forests of sixteenth-century religion, these three types may provide helpful signposts, but the tendency to regard them as rigid categories is surely to be deprecated. The century is full of individuals who flit between them and of groups incapable of bearing neat labels. As Troeltsch himself observed of his three types, 'among themselves they are strongly and variously interwoven and interconnected'.

One of the interconnections between the sectarians and the Spiritualists would seem to lie in a common medieval background. While the conventional account of Anabaptism sees it as the child of extremism in early Zwinglian Zürich, we know that many of its leaders greatly valued the *Theologia Germanica* and the writings of Johann Tauler and Thomas à Kempis. The same sources obviously lie behind the Spiritualist writers, some of whom also have clear obligations to Carlstadt and to Müntzer. More heavily than the Anabaptists, the Spiritualists turned to the tradition of Joachim of Fiore, the Spiritual Franciscans, the Beghards and the Brethren of the Free Spirit, that apocalyptic and millenarian tradition which we observed during our survey of medieval heresy. Even staider men like Osiander and Hans Sachs retained a warm interest in Joachitic literature, while Müntzer himself admitted that his teachings formed an extension from it: 'They say I received my doctrine from Abbot Joachim and call it the Eternal Gospel in ridicule. The witness of Abbot Joachim has indeed counted greatly with me, . . . but my teaching is far higher than his.' Carlstadt and Müntzer could be called both sectarians and Spiritualists; they influenced both groups. They were not purely guided by the inner light and their writings are, in Rupp's phrase, 'drenched in Scriptural quotations'. Most of the writers and preachers we call Spiritualists had something of this hybrid character, and several had passed through an Anabaptist phase which left its marks upon them. Some founded groups of devotees displaying obvious characteristics of the 'sect-type'.

DENCK, FRANCK AND SCHWENCKFELD

The spiritual religion had many centres in the cities of western and southern Germany, but its form and implications may most briefly be described if we limit our attentions to its three most remarkable writers. Hans Denck (d. 1527) was perhaps the most gifted of those who came into the movement from Anabaptism. A Bavarian of educated citizen-background and a student at Ingolstadt, he taught languages at Regensburg and worked as proof-reader for the humanist authors and printers of Basle. At Nuremberg in 1524 he was master of the St Sebaldus School, lived alongside Pirckheimer and Dürer, had close relations with Osiander. Encountering here the teachings of Carlstadt and Müntzer, he became an advocate of their views and was expelled from the city. Denck then joined Müntzer for a time at Mühlhausen and in 1525–6 lived in Augsburg, administered baptism to Hans Huth and wrote three pamphlets of importance. As the situation in Augsburg became threatening, he sought asylum in Strassburg, hitherto called by Anabaptists 'the refuge of righteousness'. Here again he was ultimately disowned by the moderates, Bucer calling him 'the Anabaptist Pope'. Banished again, he repaired to Worms, where in 1527 he produced his admirably-written tractate *Of True Love*, the tenor of which was far more mystical than Anabaptist, for his journey in the mainstream of the latter movement had proved both uneasy and brief.

In the summer of 1527 Denck, Huth and others assembled a conference in Augsburg, where they expected to figure in a second Pentecost. It was here that in the December Huth suffered imprisonment, torture and death in prison, while Denck escaped only to die soon afterwards of the plague in Basle, having made a partial recantation of his former Anabaptist views. Not yet thirty-two years of age, he had compressed the wanderings and adventures of many lifetimes into the last four years of his life. He certainly belies that neat categorization to which we have alluded.

Despite the Augsburg episode, by mental habit and behaviour Hans Denck was no fanatic. Sane, modest and sincere, he never wholly lost sight of the needs of man as understood by a humanist. He thought that Luther had liberated religion only to re-bind it in iron chains, and so restrain the progressive self-revelation of God. On the other side, he strove to draw Anabaptism towards the spiritual religion, to liberate it from its fanatical and its social-revolutionary elements. For him man was a fallen creature, yet one possessed of divine gifts and able, by the exercise of free will, to co-operate with God's ceaseless effort to save mankind. He thus denounced elective and predestinatory doctrines as involving a limitation of the love of God, who is wholly good and ordains no

111, 112 (*Left*) Title-page of the German edition of the Old Testament Prophets in which Hans Denck collaborated. The first Protestant translation, it antedates Luther's by five years. (*Right*) Title-page of Sebastian Franck's *Chronica, Zeitbuch und Geschichtbibel* (1531)

one to sin. Christ calls himself the Light of the World, yet he also uses this same expression of his disciples. Men can hence strive with some success to lessen their own selfhood and to achieve a closer harmony with the divine will. The 'inner Word' is at work in each man; the Kingdom of God is within us, and he who seeks it outside himself will never find it. Denck has no sympathy with Luther's idea of imputation: this passive reliance on the imputed merits of Christ will not suffice. No one can be called righteous unless he is righteous. Salvation is thus not a transaction performed on our behalf; it is a striving, a life, a process. Sacraments and ceremonies have little relevance to this process, but neither can a man be made righteous by the 'dead letter' of a book. The Bible itself, the 'external Word', is mainly important as witness to the more momentous 'internal Word', which increases in authenticity and power as a man succeeds in subordinating his life to the will of God.

At least equally unfettered by Catholic and Lutheran theology was Sebastian Franck (*c.* 1499–1542), a more voluminous writer and a more considerable humanist than his friend Hans Denck. He was a

145

Swabian who entered the University of Ingolstadt in 1515 and later migrated to Heidelberg, where he heard Luther defend his position in the disputations of 1518. Having accepted Catholic ordination, he soon went over to the Reformers and held a Lutheran pastorate near Nuremberg. Here he mingled with the local humanists and married Ottilie Behaim, whose artist brothers were at once pupils of Dürer, friends of Denck and sympathizers with Anabaptism. Franck's first literary work was a translation of Althamer's *Diallage*: it was a Lutheran attack on Denck and the Anabaptists, but Franck attached a preface showing strongly Spiritualist tendencies which must have jarred on the ears of Wittenberg orthodoxy. Before 1530 he was in close touch with Denck, Schwenckfeld, Bünderlin and other writers of their persuasion. In his *Chronicle of Turkey* (1530), Franck inserted passages declaring his allegiance to a spiritual, invisible, non-sectarian church:

'There are already in our times three distinct Faiths, which have a large following, the Lutheran, Zwinglian and Anabaptist; and a fourth is well on the way to birth, which will dispense with external preaching, ceremonies, sacraments, ban and office as unnecessary, and which seeks solely to gather among all peoples an invisible, spiritual Church in the unity of the Spirit and of faith, to be governed wholly by the eternal, invisible Word of God, without external means, as the apostolic Church was governed before its apostasy, which occurred after the death of the apostles.'

The following year Franck published at Strassburg a vast chronicle of Christianity (*Chronica, Zeitbuch und Geschichtbibel*). It shows little historical insight, but has interesting reflections on religious history and recent heretics, amongst whom he included Erasmus, to the latter's intense rage. The book also stresses the claims of conscience and spirit against the 'dead letter of Scripture'. The unpopularity of these views reduced him to menial work and even to periods of imprisonment, but Franck continued to expound his teaching in the *Paradoxa* of 1534 and the *Sealed Book*, written about 1539. In the latter he rejected not only narrow sectarianism but also that rigid

Christianity which would refuse to see the Jew and the Samaritan in terms of brotherhood. He valued the Platonist heritage of mysticism and said openly that Plato and Plotinus 'had spoken to him more clearly than Moses did'. While he deprecated emotional vapourings and ecstatic experiences, he held firmly to the view of earlier mysticism, that a divine element in the soul is the mark of man's dignity and the starting-point of all spiritual progress. This element he describes variously as 'spirit', 'the Word of God', 'the inner light', 'the true light'. Along with Denck, he believed in free will and in the progressive building of moral character through active co-operation with God.

Sebastian Franck's Church is in no sense localized but an invisible communion of saints. Since the death of the apostles no true external Church, no efficacious sacraments have existed. Ecclesiastical organization is better suited to children than to adults, and the Lutherans are striving in vain to reconstruct the primitive Church. Scripture itself contains much mystery, contradiction and paradox; it brings knowledge rather than the deep, self-validating experience which delivers us from sin and selfhood. We may seek the historical Jesus, but we do so in order to find Christ the eternal Word, at work throughout human life in all ages and places. The basis at least of this position lay in Eckhart, Tauler and other earlier mystics, in whose works Sebastian Franck was so well read. Yet of all the Germans he might well be regarded as the most 'modern' in his bold development of these basic ideas. He was also the most radical in applying them destructively to Catholic, Lutheran and Zwinglian theologians. In view of this situation, Franck was wise to spend his last years in liberal and kindly Basle, the city of his idol Erasmus.

The third of our major Spiritualist writers must inevitably be the Silesian aristocrat Caspar Schwenckfeld (1490–1561), who studied in Cologne, Frankfurt and Erfurt, and from 1511 seemed settled in worldly success at the little ducal court of Liegnitz. Here in Silesia the Reformation under the patronage of successive bishops of Breslau had begun before 1520. Aroused by Luther, whose personal friendship he enjoyed, Schwenckfeld soon became disillusioned by what he considered the meagre spiritual fruits of Lutheranism. 'My dear

Caspar', admitted Luther himself, 'genuine Christians are none too common. I wish I could see two together in a place.' But it was Schwenckfeld who set himself the task of rescuing Luther's world from the tendency to suppose that all spiritual problems could be solved by a mere act of faith. In 1527 the two broke apart, ostensibly over Schwenckfeld's refusal to accept consubstantiation, but really through the depth of the gulf which separated Luther from the whole Spiritualist approach. In later years Luther was discussing Schwenckfeld in robust terms: 'The stupid fool, possessed by the devil, understands nothing. . . . But if he will not stop his drivel, let him at least not pester me with the pamphlets the devil spews out of him.' Characteristically, Schwenckfeld continued to pray for Luther and to give gracious expression to his feeling of indebtedness for Luther's earlier work. From 1529, when he went into voluntary exile to prevent trouble between his friend the Duke of Liegnitz and the Silesian Lutherans, Schwenckfeld passed a wandering existence between various cities, including Strassburg, Augsburg and Ulm, at the last of which he died. Though he had no wish to found a sect, in the event he founded a tenacious one. His disciples, calling themselves Confessors of the Glory of Christ, continued in Silesia well into the nineteenth century. Meanwhile in 1734 one of their branches had crossed to Philadelphia and still survives. Schwenckfeld's writings were widely publicized by his friends and successors; they affected the Seekers of seventeenth-century England and their Dutch contemporaries the Collegiants.

The theology of Schwenckfeld adopts certain medial positions between the humanist mystics Denck and Franck on the one hand, and Lutheranism on the other. With Luther he agrees that man is wholly fallen and dead in depravity, that he possesses no natural freedom of the will, no independent ability to cast off the bonds of sin. This triumph can only arise from a supernatural act of God upon the soul. Of this activity Christ, the 'new Adam', was the first-born. By participating in his new order, by faith in Christ crucified, the human soul can be granted a rebirth, which Schwenckfeld calls the 'deification' of fallen man. Once admitted to this experience, the believer gains a new control over bodily appetites, an illumination

113 Caspar Schwenckfeld:
a late engraved portrait, 1556

of the intellect, a greater sensitivity towards sin. His transfiguration shows in his very physical aspect; even in exile and sorrow he has within him a 'castle of peace'. This is accomplished by the 'inner Word' operating upon the spiritual substance of the soul. There is a living, inner Scripture written in the believer's heart by the finger of God. The Scriptures, the 'outer Word', are valued by Schwenckfeld far above all other writings, but however powerfully they 'paint truth for the eye', they cannot alone 'bring it into the heart'. Like Denck and Franck, he insists upon depth of experience, as opposed to a mere intellectual understanding of the way of salvation. Sacramental doctrine he interprets in the light of Christ's discourse in the sixth chapter of *John*: when Christ here offers his flesh and blood to man, he is not meaning a physical sacrament but the life-giving bestowal of the Word. This is no mere symbolic transaction, but a hard fact of man's experience, his spiritual rebirth through his partaking of the nature of the glorified Christ.

THE INFLUENCE OF THE SPIRITUALISTS

These three leading writers had numerous disciples and associates, some of them, like Johann Bünderlin (d. 1533) and Christian   149

Entfelder (fl. 1526–44), men of distinction in their own right. The strange Swiss physician and neo-Platonist Paracelsus (d. 1541) has also been assigned a place in the development of Spiritualism. At another extreme but well within the tradition stands that great Dutch liberal Dirck Volckertszoon Coornheert (d. 1590), statesman, translator, engraver, friend of William the Silent, admirer of Franck and Castellio, antagonist of Calvin and forerunner of Arminianism. Together such Spiritualists form a strong connecting link between the fourteenth-century mystics and those of the seventeenth century. To Spiritualism's continuing development many forces contributed, especially those of Platonism and Cabbalistic nature-mysticism, which entered through the High Renaissance speculations of Ficino and Pico, and appear strongly in the writings of Valentin Weigel (d. 1588) and the still more famous Jakob Boehme (d. 1624). The vitality of Spiritualist beliefs throughout the seventeenth century can be seen in numerous Englishmen: John Everard, the Quakers, the Behmenists, the Cambridge Platonists and even William Law. Despite the obvious weaknesses of subjectivism, individualism, inapplicability to rank-and-file Christians, we can think of this tradition as abstracting and preserving something from the more liberal elements of three earlier movements: Catholic mysticism, Renaissance Platonism and early Protestant evangelicalism. As Jesuit-led Catholicism lost contact with the old mystical schools, as Protestantism hardened into the Lutheran, Calvinist and Anglican systems, it became important that there should survive ways of thought which valued flexibility in an ever more rigid world, and which insisted that the values of religion lay in the individual soul, not in the power and success of religious institutions.

VIII CALVIN AND GENEVA

JOHN CALVIN

Seen in retrospect, John Calvin's career has an appropriate air of inevitability. Nothing seems wasted and the man is able to secure full scope for his enormous yet distinctly circumscribed powers. From 1521, when his Picard father begged a cathedral chaplaincy to guarantee his schooling, until 1541, when he finally settled in Geneva, his experiences seem to be educating him precisely for the great task ahead. In Paris he took his Latin from the great teacher Mathurin Cordier and like Luther began his philosophy and theology under Nominalist influences. At Orleans and Bourges he not only acquired a valuable legal training but learned Greek and attracted notice as one of the more accomplished young humanists of his day. When his father died in 1531 he felt free to relinquish the law, return to Paris and apply himself anew to linguistic, classical and biblical studies. His first book was a commentary on Seneca's *De Clementia*, a work significant for him, as also for Zwingli, through its Stoic moral teaching. Aside from the congenial lessons of this philosophy, Calvin's humanism was more a matter of technical equipment than one of fundamental outlook: it developed his superlative gift for exact, lucid, unadorned yet elegant statement both in Latin and in French.

His crucial experience is described with characteristic restraint in the preface to his *Commentary on the Psalms*: 'By a sudden conversion, God subdued and reduced to docility my soul, which was more hardened against such things than one would expect of my youthful years.' He does not date this event, but it probably occurred towards the end of 1533, about the time of his personal involvement in the struggle of the Reformation. On All Saints' Day in that year his intimate friend Nicholas Cop, recently made rector of the University of Paris, ventured to deliver an oration approving Lutheran

114, 115 This most recently discovered portrait (anonymous) of the young Calvin (*left*) shows him as he was on the eve of his arrival in Geneva. The city he saw was not sub-

views on justification. Amongst those who followed Cop in precipitate flight was Calvin, who probably lay already under suspicion, since his rooms were searched and his papers confiscated within a few hours of his disappearance. There followed many hazardous months of provincial travel under an assumed name, during which he met Lefèvre and many others of the French Reformers. Reaching Basle in February 1535, he arranged for the publication of his *Institutes of the Christian Religion*, a stout Latin primer or catechism in six chapters, dedicated with great elegance and greater optimism to the King of France. In the second edition of 1539 it was enlarged almost threefold and better arranged. This process continued more slowly in subsequent editions, culminating in the definitive version of 1559, with its four books divided into eighty chapters. The series of editions in French began in 1541 and was destined to exercise a major influence upon French prose literature to the time of Bossuet.

In the summer of 1535 Calvin took advantage of a temporary respite given to French heretics; he revisited France to settle family affairs and bring out a younger brother and sister. Wishing to withdraw to Strassburg, he found the armies of Francis and Charles across his route and hence planned a detour through Geneva. This fateful circumstance led to his meeting there with the firebrand Guillaume Farel (1489–1565), who with a flash of inspiration

stantially smaller than when this scene was drawn at the end of the century. The Cathedral of Saint Peter (*right*) dominated a lakeside metropolis of some 16,000 inhabitants

adjured him to stay and complete the work of Reformation in the city. This proposition might have daunted the boldest zealot. We have already observed the dangerous suspension of Geneva between the opposing poles of Savoy and Berne. A restive community of some 16,000 inhabitants, it had revolted against its overlord the bishop, who backed his fulminations by troops borrowed from his friend the Duke of Savoy. Apart from their alliance with Berne, the Protestant Genevans had few sources of strength. That the citizens were exceptionally divided and turbulent appears throughout their whole history almost to the time of Calvin's death in 1564. Many of the so-called 'Libertines' deserved their title in no mere ecclesiastical sense, and their notoriety does not rest on Calvin's witness alone. Whatever the situation elsewhere in Switzerland, Calvin did not in Geneva itself enter upon any comfortable inheritance from Zwingli.

After a couple of years his first attempt to control the situation ended disastrously, when he and Farel refused to adopt a Bernese liturgy accepted over their heads by the council of Geneva. Dismissed from his pastorate, Calvin fruitfully spent the years 1538–41 in the very different atmosphere of Strasburg, where he ministered to the French congregation and learned a great deal about international Protestantism. Here Martin Bucer taught him more than any other. His debts to Bucer became specific as well as general, for Bucer stood among those theologians who anticipated Calvin in

153

their stress on the doctrine of predestination and their desire to give it a precise meaning in relation to a redeeming Christ. Bucer also preceded Calvin in his concern for the rehabilitation of the ministry and in envisaging it as a fourfold body of pastors, teachers, elders and deacons. A creative liturgist, he furnished prototypes of the simpler ceremonies later offered by Calvin to Geneva. Nevertheless, Calvin took from Bucer, as from any source, precisely what he needed for his own scheme, and he translated everything into his personal idioms of thought and style. His idioms differed radically from those of the German theologians, who were so often verbose and untidy to the point of inconsistency. A much less important event of Calvin's Strassburg years was his marriage, yet compared with Luther's it symbolizes the swift-changing nature of the age. Whereas Katherine von Bora was an ex-nun, Idelette de Bure was the widow of an Anabaptist.

Protesting that death was preferable to resuming his cross at Geneva, Calvin nevertheless accepted the call to return as coming from God. He neither returned in triumph nor exercised anything like a dictatorship. For many years he was little more than the leading minister of this faction-ridden community, and even when he had become an oracle throughout the great Protestant world, the Genevan city council remained capable of overruling his wishes and those of the whole pastorate, even on spiritual matters. The recently-published register of the Geneva Company of Pastors has served to emphasize this aspect of his situation. On his deathbed Calvin recalled to his fellow-ministers the bitterness of his struggles amidst this 'perverse and ill-natured people'. But he concluded: 'God has given me the power to write. . . . I have written nothing in hatred . . . but always I have faithfully attempted what I believed to be for the glory of God.' Amid all his tribulations, at least Luther's demon of doubt seems to have spared him. His conversion had left him sure that he had been fashioned by God into an instrument of the divine will, that God in his inscrutable wisdom had condescended to use Calvin's reasoning powers to restore truth to the human race. A modern observer might well feel dismayed by his blend of humility with a sense of unique vocation. Yet he belonged to an age when men still

116 Martin Bucer: engraved portrait by René Boivin, 1544

117 Guillaume Farel: this anonymous portrait shows him in later life as the minister of Neuchâtel

believed in prophets and saints; he was exceptional not so much in his claim to a divine commission as in the outstanding intelligence of his methods. He knew how and when to become flexible over details while rigidly pursuing his main objectives. A practical negotiator as well as a natural scholar and synthesist, he possessed little of the common touch, the wayward and original genius of Luther. Yet the elements of his theology are with few exceptions based upon the work of Luther, whom he regarded with an unswerving veneration. He sought to rescue Luther's doctrine from sectarian hands, from what he called the *esprits phrénétiques*, and in later years from the narrowness of those who had made themselves the guardians of Lutheran orthodoxy. Unlike Luther, he was not prepared to adopt an attitude of simple trust and leave everything to the Word, for he saw himself and his own system as strenuous agents of the Word. Above all, he sought to embody Luther's teaching in a Church and in a society which would really put that teaching into practice.

CALVINIST TEACHINGS

Summaries of Calvin's theological system rightly stress its intense biblicism and its resolute theocentricity, but these ideas require

155

careful qualification. As the greatest biblical theologian of his age, Calvin was no mere fundamentalist. He doubted the authenticity of 2 *Peter*, *James* and *Jude*; and if he dismissed Castellio for insisting that the *Canticles* were Hebrew love-poetry, he accepted like any other humanist the need for historical and textual criticism. He saw the Bible as the sole reliable authority for our knowledge of God. Without attempting to accord equal weight to every passage of the Scriptures, he regarded the will of God as immutable and Christ as operating timelessly in both Testaments. Hence he gave the Old Testament a normative function almost equal to that of the New, and he did not stress with Luther our delivery from Old Law into the glorious liberty of the Gospel. He says austerely that 'the exemption which Christ has procured for us does not imply that we no longer owe any obedience to the doctrine of the law'. While he sometimes seems to regard the biblical writers as amanuenses of the Holy Spirit, he did not for one moment suppose that the Bible obviated the need for a strong Church. Again, he believed in the corroborative witness of the Holy Spirit within the hearts of those who read the Bible. The authenticating Spirit and the Scriptures are thus two aspects of God's self-revealing process, the Word. Naturally, this sober notion differs greatly from inward authentication as envisaged by the Spiritualists. To Calvin all mystics were vainglorious Prometheans storming heaven by means of human scaling-ladders. The Word was neither a book nor an inner light, but an interaction of both under the power of the Holy Spirit.

Despite the debt of his Geneva to the Zürich model, Calvin regarded Zwingli as a second-rate theologian and often diverged from him. The core of Calvin's teaching was directly inherited from Luther and some of its refinements from Bucer. That core lies in its theocentric character, in its insistence on magnifying the sovereignty and providence of God, the source of all reality. Set in a profound and impenetrable mystery, the Divine Will dominates all persons and things. Calvin is primarily concerned with this vision of the nature of God, less with the theory of man's predestination. Of the latter he had little to say in 1536; if later on he came to say more, this was largely through pastoral and polemical reasons rather than through any desire to make predestination the nucleus of his system. Ere long the anthropocentric aspect unduly attracted Calvin's successors and they, concerned and curious over the human predicament, upset the balance of his scheme.

This said, we should nevertheless resist the tendency to soften the message of Calvin, who taught predestinatory doctrine with a more frank and uncompromising logic than any of his several distinguished predecessors. This all-sufficient God governs 'not only heaven and earth and inanimate creatures', but also 'the counsels and wills of men . . . so as to move precisely to that end directed by him'. Man has fallen wholly into corruption and self-centredness; he can achieve no jot of justification and salvation by his own efforts. If God elects us to salvation, 'ce n'est pas pour nos beaux yeux'. We are all undeserving, and if God assigns only some of us to his reprobation and punishment, this cannot be called injustice. Yet Calvin was no revivalist vulgarian; he regarded hell-fire as a metaphor expressing the dreadful plight of those forever deprived of God's presence.

The notion that Calvin was the last of the great scholastics, the author of a tightly-jointed *summa theologica*, is apt to encourage superficial and misleading inferences. Though he incurred some debts to Duns Scotus and the Nominalists, he drew all his essentials from the Bible, which he read with Augustine and Luther ever in mind. Moreover his logic and consistency have sometimes been accorded excessive veneration. The arguments purporting to link the utter sovereignty of the Creator with the utter corruption of the creature might well be regarded as sophistries which no dogmatic phrases, no appeal to mystery will suffice to cover. And when told that God uses this arbitrary, selective salvation as a means to prove his mercy, we are again entitled to remain unconvinced. So far as these transactions are concerned, Calvin's God is indeed as remote, inscrutable, alien, deficient in fatherly love as the God we see in nature. And though Christ called many but chose few, a series of arbitrary sentences to eternal and punitive damnation cannot securely be based upon the wholeness of his recorded teaching. Even so, no summary does Calvin justice. The reader tired of textbooks will find it far more rewarding to take up a good English translation and work through a few chapters—perhaps the four dealing with predestination (*Institutes of the Christian Religion*, III, 21-4). We who do not share Calvin's premises or his method cannot withhold our tribute to this splendid adroitness, this remorseless efficiency with which he applies and groups the relevant passages of Scripture. This is an intellectual performance of the first order, one which must have seemed overwhelming amid the relative simplicities of sixteenth-century exegesis.

It was Calvin's distinction, not to conduct impeccable chains of argument to invincible conclusions, but rather to confront orthodox Christian thought with its supreme antinomies, to explore its many paradoxes in the light of the Bible. This he did with more honesty and learning than any of his rivals, though like the rest he can hardly be exonerated from the charge of going to the Bible to prove positions he had already selected. Having done all this, he either swept the unresolved elements under the carpet of mystery or left them lying about the room to trouble us. Like Luther, he deprecated the notion that men could obtain knowledge of salvation by seeking to probe ever more deeply into the hidden laws of God. Instead, they should live in hope, sustained by the inward assurance born of personal fellowship with Christ. And it is Luther again whom Calvin echoes in saying that no man can judge whether others be among the elect: 'The eyes of God alone see who will endure to the end.' The true Church of the elect is thus invisible. When in the real world Calvin's followers needed tests for Church-membership, he advised them to proceed with tolerance and charity. People should be deemed elect of God and members of his Church if 'by confession of faith, by exemplary life, and participation in the sacraments, they profess with us the same God and Christ'. On the other side, disbelievers, nominal Christians and persons of evil life should be held non-members of the Church *for the present*. If the Church excommunicates, it makes no presumptuous suggestion that the people excommunicated will fail to attain salvation. Calvin was under no illusion that Christ had commissioned churchmen with final powers to manipulate divine justice.

Apart from this vision of God's majesty and his great machine of election and reprobation, there is another and more approachable

118, 119 New directions in Christian doctrine and liturgy: the title-page of the final revision of the *Institutes of the Christian Religion* (Geneva, Estienne, 1559) and part of the Calvinist setting for Clément Marot's Penitential Psalms, No. 137—'By the waters of Babylon'

Calvin to whom attention is increasingly paid. He is not merely a theocentric but a Christocentric thinker, Christ being the key-figure of his cosmic drama and faith in Christ the mark of the elect. He is vitally concerned with divine mercy and redemptive power, as well as with the more fearful aspects of the divine plan. To neglect these moving, impressive passages would be to barbarize a great theologian and reduce him to the level of his least enlightened followers.

Calvin was a second-generation Reformer, attacking problems different from those which had confronted Luther twenty years earlier. On Luther's own showing, the Word had proved anything but irresistible, and there now succeeded men anxious to create and to operate ecclesiastical, social and even political mechanisms which would at least attack corrupting influences and help to clear the channels for the operation of the divine grace. Amongst these activist churchmen, Calvin was the greatest, whether judged by his intellectual achievement or by the impact of his system upon Europe. While he insisted that the visible Church must not seek to usurp God's prerogatives, he nevertheless plunged ever more deeply into the practical organization of local churches, and into defining the functions of the whole Church. In a famous passage near the opening of the fourth book, he says bluntly: 'There is no entering into life unless the Church conceives us in her womb, brings us to birth, nourishes us at her bosom and preserves us by her guardianship and discipline . . . no forgiveness of sins is to be hoped for beyond her embrace, nor any salvation.' God alone is the source of our redemption, but in history and in practice he redeems through the fellowship and discipline of the Church.

The structure of Calvin's Church was not governed by a narrow literalism. By 1541 he was propounding the fourfold ministry of pastors, teachers, deacons, and a college of elders, a scheme which represented a bold modification of the biblical sources and could function either openly or implicitly as part of a chain of command. Calvin had in fact no invincible objections to the name and functions of a bishop. He lectured Archbishop Cranmer on the high obligations of his office and he approved a scheme of bishops to be instituted by his followers in Poland. So far as concerned forms of worship, he accepted like Melanchthon the liberal notion that many usages are *adiaphora* or things indifferent, having no title to be universally imposed. He recognized the need for flexible manoeuvre and often enough he urged zealots to advance slowly.

In regard to the vexed problems of the Lord's Supper Calvin refused Catholic transubstantiation, Lutheran consubstantiation and Zwinglian symbolism alike. Despite his caution over frontal clashes with Wittenberg, he refuted the Lutheran belief in the ubiquity of Christ's body as an unnecessary hypothesis. This action led him into harsh controversy with the able Lutheran Joachim Westphal, pastor of Hamburg, who took full advantage of the ambiguities in Calvin's sacramental teaching. In the *Institutes* Calvin says he finds no inconsistency in accepting here a mystery: 'I rather experience than understand it.' In his *Petite Traicté de la Cène* (1542) he would 'exclude all carnal imagination', and he bids his readers lift their hearts to heaven, 'not supposing that our Lord Jesus could so descend as to be enclosed within corruptible elements'. On the other hand, by a holy mystery, 'the spirit of God is the means of our partaking,

120 German satire on the Calvinist Lord's Supper: detail from a large engraving published by Johann Krell in the middle of the century, on the history of all heretical errors concerning the communion sacrament. One portion of the engraving celebrates those who have defended the sacrament; there comes at the end of a long procession 'a man dear to God and the last of the German prophets, Doctor Martin Luther'. In the portion reproduced here the Calvinist celebrant, pumped with hot air by a devil, is made to say 'Take eat, in memory only.' And below: 'I, Satan, am also among the Calvinists.'

which is therefore said to be a spiritual partaking'. This dual notion of a spiritual presence linked with a bodily ceremony was largely derived from Bucer; it had affinities also with the belief independently adopted about 1546 by Ridley and Cranmer from their study of the ninth-century theologian Ratramnus of Corbie.

Calvin produced a simplified and closely Scriptural order of communion. He left no doubt as to the primacy of the Word over the sacraments, which in his view announce and manifest grace but do not bestow it. Salvation could be achieved even without sacraments. Having, however, erected such safeguards against the Catholics, Calvin accorded a high place to the Supper in the life of the Church, and he urged that it should be celebrated at least once a week. It was in fact the obduracy of the Geneva council which limited celebrations to four in the year. This clash with the magistrates was by no means unique, yet on the whole Calvin asserted the independence of the Church with more success than the other Reformers. Unlike Luther, he believed that the Church must manage her own affairs while yet maintaining an active partnership with the State. The Church should permeate with her insight the whole of society and especially the magistrates. The secular government had nevertheless been ordained by God, while the civil magistrate, having a divine vocation, protected standards of morality decreed by God. Princes must be obeyed even while they oppress, though sometimes divine authority may be claimed for action, duly guided by inferior magistrates, against a heretical or infidel sovereign who confronts his people with the stark choice between wholesale apostasy and rebellion. Oppressive rulers cannot without sin be resisted forcibly by private citizens. While, however, it is true that Calvin's view cannot lightly be equated with those of later Calvinism, in the present writer's impression the standard accounts do not take seriously enough the loopholes left by him to the political activists. He admits (*Inst.* IV, 20, 30) that God sometimes commissions avenging prophets like Moses, a more than academic exception in an age which had not relegated prophets to the past. Again Calvin indicates (*Inst.* IV, 20, 31) that certain inferior magistrates, like the ephors of Sparta and the tribunes of Rome, have a positive duty to take the lead in opposing tyrants, and he appears to ascribe a similar function to modern Estates. In 1559 he even speaks of a biblical king as having 'virtually abnegated his power' by exalting his authority above that of God. From all men (*Inst.* IV, 20, 32) he demands passive disobedience to commands manifestly against the divine law. In a letter of 1561 to Coligny he countenances resistance to the King of France, should this be agreed upon by the Princes of the Blood and the Parlements. In short, however reluctantly Calvin allowed exceptions to the rule of non-resistance, he surely said enough to encourage men who did not share his scruples.

THE GENEVAN EXPERIMENT

In Geneva a disciplinary ideal was laid down by the Church ordinances of 1541 and outwardly it had been realized by Calvin's later years. The pastors, men of manifest orthodoxy and integrity, were to meet every Friday for scriptural exercises. In two of the three city churches Sunday sermons were delivered at dawn; at all three churches again at nine o'clock. At noon came the catechizing of the young and at three a further sermon. In addition, sermons were preached on three weekdays, and finally every day. The pastors appointed deacons to visit the sick and relieve the poor. The twelve elders, chosen from the municipal councils and so linking Church and State, collaborated with the pastors in the Consistory, which met every Thursday under the presidency of one of the syndics to supervise the moral life of the city. The surviving minutes of the Consistory show it forbidding dances, ostentatious costume and lewd songs, reproving the mildest superstitions, punishing frauds and overcharges. Adulterers repeatedly suffered the death penalty and on one occasion a young person was beheaded for striking his parents. Like the lawyer he had been, Calvin sought to demarcate the boundaries of ecclesiastical and secular jurisdiction, yet each constantly impinged upon the other. The city government saw to the efficiency of the pastors and even regulated the length of their sermons. On the other hand, the Consistory often gave advice on economic matters, including rates of interest and the control of prices. Calvin himself helped to revise the municipal code—and even to improve methods of refuse-disposal! In 1546 he persuaded the council to replace the taverns by evangelical places of refreshment, where bawdy entertainment and light conversation were banned, where a Bible had to be available for consultation and where no meal could be served until grace had been said. Predictably enough, these decorous establishments failed to yield profits and were again replaced by taverns. Calvin was no philistine but a discriminating lover of poetry and music; he also approved the plastic arts within what he considered their proper sphere, but his concept of the divine majesty made him denounce the attempts of artists to depict God in human form.

It remains, of course, disputable whether Calvin raised Genevan personal morality to a higher level than that of other cities. Some observers thought his Geneva a model community; others found evidence of much vice and laxity under the veneer of godliness. The records do not indicate that serious offences declined, while the death penalty continued to be exacted with a frequency remarkable even in that age. Like later Puritan governments, that of Geneva displayed an increased ferocity towards witches, of whom on the average two or three were burned every year. Yet if Geneva failed to become a Protestant *civitas Dei*, its way of life offered advantages as well as restrictions. It allowed laymen a more creative part in Church affairs than they had enjoyed in earlier times. It became a clean and orderly town in which the poor, the aged and the sick were well tended and where educational opportunity became excellent. Through Calvin's indefatigable efforts, the university was founded in 1559 with Theodore Beza (1519–1605) as its first head. It swiftly won distinction, assisted by a mass-resignation of the Lausanne professoriate, which quarrelled with the council of that town and migrated to Geneva. Altogether, life in the city of Calvin must be measured alongside the fact that many men positively enjoyed long sermons. In the last resort we mislead ourselves if we concentrate overmuch upon compulsions unacceptable to modern liberalism. The burning of Servetus might embarrass the Calvinists in tolerant Poland and elicit a few protests from advanced liberals elsewhere, but it was approved by the respectable people of both Catholic and Protestant Europe. It tells us little about the special qualities of the Genevan experiment. When John Knox called Geneva 'the most perfect school of Christ that ever was in earth since the days of the Apostles', he did well to use the word 'school', for Calvinism sought with all its might to discipline by teaching and persuasion. It fell back on excommunication and civil penalties when the gentler weapons had failed after repeated and pertinacious effort. An activist creed naturally sought intelligent co-operation rather than blind or unwilling obedience. In Calvin's later years, this outlook had become part of the energetic spirit of the age. Despite the Inquisition, a reformed Catholicism was now pursuing remedies based on education and propaganda, remedies administered by a new sort of clergy, armed also with a formidable training and earning by actual performance their high prestige.

121 About two years before Calvin's death a student, Jacques Bourgoing de Nevers, sketched him lecturing, in his copy of Gaguin's *History of France*

CALVINISM'S INTERNATIONAL APPEAL

The Reformed religion had some characteristics of the 'sect-type', yet it sprang from a mind with broad and even ecumenical aspirations. In subscribing with Bullinger to the Zürich Agreement of 1549, Calvin tolerated phrases which he would never have chosen on his own initiative, phrases purely aimed to conciliate Zwinglian opinion and so to unite all Swiss Protestants in one Reformed faith. To the end of his life he strove to achieve a similar agreement with the Lutherans and the decline of his once cordial relations with Melanchthon cannot be blamed upon him. He never reconciled himself to failure on this front. He believed in the future triumph of a world-wide Church and backed the scheme of 1556 to send a mission to Brazil. On the essential brotherhood of the whole human race, he expressed strangely liberal sentiments. 'We cannot but behold our own face in those who are poor and despised . . . even though they are utter strangers to us.' Even a Moor or a barbarian 'from the very fact of his being a man', carries about with him 'a mirror in which we can see he is our brother and our neighbour'. And no English student of Protestant history can help contrasting the warmth of the reception which he accorded our Marian exiles with the cold caution shown by nearly all the Lutheran communities.

If we planned to chronicle the expansion, the triumphs and the disasters of Calvinism, we should need to follow the mainstream of European history at least to the Peace of Westphalia. In the context of the decades which followed the mid-century, Calvinism became better equipped for expansion than its Lutheran or its radical rivals. Its teachings were more readily intelligible and systematic than those of Wittenberg; it demanded to be taken as a whole and lent itself less easily to the disputes of rival princes and their court theologians.

Among non-Germans at least, the Reformed religion proved more appealing than the Evangelical once it could compete on reasonably level terms. It proved especially seductive to intelligent, industrious, order-loving townsmen and even to that fast-multiplying class of landowners, which invested where possible in lands taken from the Church and which saw land in terms of peace, order and profit.

FRANCE AND THE NETHERLANDS

Those two great conflicts, the French Wars of Religion and the Revolt of the Netherlands, had close links with each other, religious, military and ideological. Moreover, both were firmly connected back to Geneva. From that source both Huguenots and Dutch patriots derived inspiration for their leaders, their synodal organization, the basis of their theories of resistance. To both movements princely leadership was as vital as to the Lutherans, and it was forthcoming from Louis, Duke of Condé and from William of Orange. Yet while both these men accepted conversion to Calvinism, neither was a devout pietist. It is rather among their lieutenants, the diplomats and propagandists, among men like Theodore Beza and Philip Marnix van Sint Aldegonde (1538–98), that we find daily links between these princes and the rigours of the Calvinist world.

From 1555 the missionaries who went into France were trained, examined for proficiency, and furnished with testimonials by the Geneva company of pastors. In 1557 the same company made the first of its many appointments to pastorates in the Netherlands, though for this field the University of Heidelberg also afforded an important training-ground. The Reformed churches exerted more distinctly political and military influences. In 1560–1 the synods of south-west France mustered troops with the local churches and regional colloquies as recruiting units, and their activity explains why Condé could gather so large a force so quickly, when in 1562 open revolt developed. Likewise in 1566 the Calvinist consistories meeting in Antwerp attempted to set up an entire military general staff, to be headed by Orange. We have already observed that even Calvin envisaged the possibility that 'inferior' magistrates might lawfully resist tyrannical or godless rulers. And when asked to identify

122 Theodore Beza:
engraved portrait
by J. Hogenberg, 1595

these privileged inferiors, Calvinist theory could adapt its answers to each local situation: they could be the Estates, the Princes of the Blood, even humble city magistrates. Hence both Genevan agents and theories alike had much to do with these two great explosions of the later sixteenth century. Geneva supplied the current and the wires which led to the plentiful local stores of dynamite.

Besides the aristocratic leadership and the Genevan pastorate, the Calvinist parties in the Netherlands and in France contained more democratic elements combining economic grievances with real religious convictions. Such were the anticlerical merchants, the artisans and small shopkeepers labouring under war taxation and rising prices, sailors and shipbuilders affected by rebellion and privateering, weavers and labourers hit by unemployment and repressive guild-controls, small squires lacking regular military employment and faced by the effect of inflation on their static landed incomes. During the 'sixties and 'seventies such elements spearheaded those myriad local movements of subversion whereby Calvinism through force and political intrigue took over so many French and Netherlandish towns. The Sea Beggars who organized the Dutch Revolt abroad and returned to revitalize it were among the most ruthless and democratic of these groups. In both France and the Netherlands truly revolutionary parties had come to birth. Unlike medieval rebels, unlike the more recent Anabaptists, these men for a

123 This anti-Huguenot lampoon depends on a pun—*baiser*—on the name of Theodore Beza, or *de Bèze*. Calvin is the donkey on which the miller rides to the *moulin de malencontre*

125 Calvin caricatured in 1566 by Arcimboldi

124 Huguenots as apes, traditional symbol of profanity

126 Iconoclasm in the Netherlands: engraving from Baron Eytzinger's *De Leone Belgico*, published at Cologne, 1583. Statues are being toppled (one lies already in the porch), stained glass systematically broken; even the clerical casks are being smashed (far right)

time transcended class-barriers in the common cause, and the force which bound together their hitherto divergent interests and discontents was the Calvinist religion. A little later militant Catholicism imitated this feat among the Leaguers of France. These complexities and comparisons have recently been analysed by Professor Koenigsberger with a detail we cannot here follow. He has also stressed the temporary character of the Calvinist bond and the toughness of the traditional ruling classes both in town and country. When the Dutch Revolt had won so much of the Netherlands as military factors allowed, when the Huguenots had put Henry of Navarre on the throne and won their cities of refuge, then the old leadership reasserted itself, the democratic elements once more conformed, and society eschewed those radical changes of structure which had seemed imminent during the years of crisis. Far-reaching political and religious changes had been accomplished without social revolution.

127 A service in the Lyon Temple, called 'Paradise': anonymous painting of 1564. The sexes are segregated, and there is a clear distinction of rank in the seating. The preacher, hatted in the Calvinist manner, is timed by an hourglass. Despite the sparse attendance indicated, Lyons had one of the earliest and strongest congregations in France

Despite these and other common features, the two great movements steadily diverged. In the Netherlands the ultimate appearance of a Protestant North and a Catholic South was occasioned by the brute facts of geography and military history, not by cultural and religious differentials. Previous to the Revolt and during its early stages, Calvinism won its main successes in Antwerp, Ghent and other southern cities. It seems appropriate enough that the Antwerper Pieter Brueghel best illustrated the period of field preachers and inquisitors, and had to destroy some of his pictures as Alva's persecution developed. Yet it was in Zeeland and Holland that the Sea Beggars could capture a strong chain of bases, while the geographically defenceless South fell victim to the generalship of Parma. During the 'eighties the torch had been handed on from conquered Flanders and Brabant to Holland and Zeeland, which, ensconced

130 The Massacre of St Bartholomew in Paris, August 24, 1572: painting by François Dubois d'Amiens, a reputed eye-witness. The artist has included (right centre) the young Charles IX inspecting the decapitated body of the Protestant leader Coligny. Catherine de Medici (left background) examines some of her calculated handiwork ▶

128 John the Baptist as a field preacher, by Brueghel: he addresses what is evidently a contemporary Protestant outdoor meeting

129 (*Left*) Hercules slaying the Hydra: the official version from a medal struck by the King's order to celebrate the massacre of 1572

behind a formidable barrier of floods and estuaries, founded the nucleus of the new Dutch Republic. Amid these events, the manifest attributes of clear belief, good discipline and unyielding persistence had brought the Calvinist minority to the leadership of the revolt and to the control of the churches. Throughout the dark days of 1572–4, 1584–5 and 1587–8 their zeal inspired even those of the patriots who did not share their creed. Yet even in 1600 only about half the population of Holland and Zeeland had become Calvinist. Throughout the other provinces the Reformed religion embraced minorities until well into the seventeenth century. Less than a tenth of the Catholic clergy went over to Protestantism, while the mood of a very large section of the mercantile patriciate remained coolly Erasmian rather than warmly Calvinist. And while in 1618–19 the strict Calvinists were destined to win the struggle at the Synod of Dort, they then signally failed to dominate either the Arminian regent class or the expanding cultural life of the golden age. Dutch Calvinism had spent all too much of its spiritual vitality in the actual winning of freedom from Spain.

131 Spanish troops leaving the city of Maastricht, 1577: engraving from Baron Eytzinger's *De Leone Belgico*, 1583. They would soon return after the short-lived détente of that year

In the crucial enterprise of France the situation proved even more complex. We have already enumerated some of those factors in French politics and society which discouraged the early advances of Protestantism. Against these the Genevan religion had to contend in its turn, though in relation to France it could boast some peculiar advantages. Its doctrine was stated by the greatest French theologian of the age and with a full mastery of the French tongue. In the metrical psalms of Clément Marot, which attained over fifty editions between 1543 and 1563, it found a devotional instrument of enormous popular appeal. A large part of the recruits to its ministry were Frenchmen, who naturally returned to win their own country: in the three years 1559–61 Geneva sent at least 120 ministers into France alone. Already in 1555 the Paris congregation had a resident pastor and four years later, when the first national synod met in the capital, no less than 72 local churches sent representatives. By 1561 Admiral Coligny was claiming that 2,150 congregations existed.

The extent to which regional economic and social trends affected the fortunes of the movement has become a notable theme of modern historical research. It has been observed that the 'continental' cities of France—Troyes, Tours, Bourges, and especially Lyons— were inclining around the mid-century towards economic and intellectual stagnation. On the other hand the rise of overseas commerce was lending a new impetus to the ports and maritime zones of the west and the north. To some degree this 'outward tilt' corresponded with, and perhaps affected, the religious history of France. The 'continental' sectors, once so open to Lutheranism, apparently hardened against Protestant ideas. In particular, Champagne and Burgundy fell under the influence of the reactionary Guise family and along with the Guise duchy of Lorraine became a part of the great Counter-Reformation corridor stretching from Italy to the southern Netherlands. Meanwhile, it was mainly in the maritime provinces that the Huguenots after 1569 built up their cities of refuge together with the famous cavalry corps upon which their prowess in arms depended.

Though it seems clear that Huguenotism received stimulus from the general *malaise économique*, neat and rigid theories of economic causation must be regarded with great caution. In this profoundly provincial society of France, family and personal influences—from those of Bourbon, Guise and Montmorency downward—bore heavy weight in every part of the country. Such problems will long remain subject to local researches, yet faced by this whirlpool of secular forces and motives, we are doubtless justified in regarding the label 'French Wars of Religion' as a truly alarming simplification. Certainly the involved struggle continued long after the period now under discussion, and its outcome was notably inconclusive. Even so, the failure of Calvinism to realize its brilliant hopes of 1560 remains the salient outcome. As early as 1569 the Venetian ambassador thought that its resort to force and its acts of iconoclasm had alienated a population hitherto favourably disposed. By 1588 the astute Duc de Nevers asserted that Huguenotism was rapidly losing its ability to make fresh converts. Even as the Huguenots were allowed to become a state within a state, they had passed their zenith in French society. After a period of moderate handling by the crown, it was left to the crass bigotry of Louis XIV to abandon, or rather to postpone, the assimilation of their energies into the national life of France.

SCOTLAND, GERMANY AND EASTERN EUROPE

Under the far simpler circumstances of Scotland, the Calvinism of John Knox enlisted in 1559–60 the support of the Lords of the Congregation and the common people, placing itself at the head of a movement of national self-determination. Here again may be observed, especially in the exchanges between Knox and Maitland of Lethington, that familiar tension between religious revolution from below and the struggle of the nobles to retain governmental and social power. Throughout the remainder of the century the fortunes of Scottish Presbyterianism underwent many vicissitudes, yet its hold was gradually consolidated at all levels. In no other country did Calvinism mould so forcibly the powers and the limitations of a people, while its independent dynamic was nowhere better displayed than in that supreme irony: the vital contribution made by the Scots to the downfall of their Stuarts in England.

THE
APPELLATION
OF
JOHN KNOX,

From the cruell and most unjust Sentence pronounced against him, by the false Bishops and Clergie
of *Scotland:* With his Supplication and Exhortation to the Nobility, States, and Com-
munalty of the same Realme.

To the Nobility and States of SCOTLAND,
JOHN KNOX *wisheth Grace, Mercy and Peace, from God the Father of our
Lord Jesus Christ, with the Spirit of righteous Judgement.*

T is not onely the love of this Temporall
life (Right Honourable) neither yet the
fear of Corporal death, that moveth me
at this present to expose unto you the in-
juries done against me, and to crave of
you, as of lawfull Powers by God appointed, redresse of the same; But partly it proceedeth from that reverence
which every man oweth to Gods Eter-
nall Truth: And partly, from a love
which I bear to your Salvation, and to
the Salvation of my Brethren abused in
that Realme, by such as have no fear of
God before their eyes. It hath pleased God of his infinite mercy, not
onely to illuminate the eyes of my minde, and so to touch my dull heart,
that cleerly I see, and by his grace unfainedly believe, That there is no
other name given to men under the heaven in which Salvation consisteth,
save

LLl 3

132, 133 The *Appellation* of John Knox against the censure of the Scottish Church.
The portrait of Knox (*right*) was engraved by Hondius

In Germany Calvinism confronted the formidable spectre of
Luther: a popular movement developed only in the north-western
Rhineland and in Westphalia, both areas being influenced by the
neighbouring Netherlands. In 1563 the Elector Frederick III of the
Palatinate accepted the Reformed religion and made Heidelberg its
leading German intellectual centre, while soon afterwards a lesser
focus was created by the House of Orange in Nassau. The city of
Bremen also threw in its lot with Calvinism and later on there were
princely converts like John Sigismund of Brandenburg, but outside
these limited areas Calvinism achieved no deep social penetration.
Its greatest German political philosopher Johannes Althusius (1557–
1638) might express some of its more democratic ideas, but in the
real world German Calvinism had to accept, alongside a somewhat
modified Genevan theology, the older Lutheran patterns in Church
and State.

In Poland and Hungary Calvinism profited from some very
different circumstances. The Polish and Magyar gentries sent many
of their sons to the German and Swiss Protestant universities, but
they were Latin-educated and found the Teutonic flavour of

175

Lutheranism unseductive. Still less did they relish its apotheosis of monarchs, since they themselves were striving to dominate their respective nations. The fact that Calvinism granted so large a share in the election of pastors and the management of churches to lay elders attracted these aristocrats even more than it attracted the gentry of France. Calvinist local and regional organization provided the type of ecclesiastical framework through which they could best extend their control of local, provincial and national institutions. In Poland they systematically embraced the task of proselytization; several even operated printing presses on their estates for this purpose.

The real directors of Polish Calvinism were not the foreign missionaries, but great landowners like the Radziwills and native divines like John à Lasco (1499–1560). After some eventful years in England and Germany the last-named returned in 1557 and devoted his later years to the organization of a Polish national Church. By that date a fully-fledged Presbyterianism existed in Little Poland, but while Lithuania followed suit, in Great Poland and Prussia the Lutherans and the Bohemian Brethren remained powerful. Both Sigismund Augustus (1548–72) and Stephen Báthory (Prince of Transylvania from 1571 and King of Poland, 1575–86) were highly liberal Catholic monarchs, who mixed on friendly terms with their Protestant subjects. Correctly interpreting the independent temper of the Poles, they made their country the most tolerant in Europe. The promising experiment in mutual toleration agreed on at the Conference of Warsaw in 1573 was destined to impermanence through disunity between the Protestant churches, still more through the gradual triumph of the Jesuits, who by the end of the seventeenth century made Poland one of the most Catholic countries of Europe. St Peter Canisius reconnoitred the country as early as 1558 and despatched the first successful Jesuit missionaries some seven years later.

Meanwhile in Hungary a similar Calvinist combination had won over a large part of the country, though an appreciable share was also taken by the town of Debrecen, the 'Hungarian Geneva'. Converted by Mátyás Bíró, this place was ruled for a quarter of a century by its formidable bishop Peter Juhász, who ensured that the

Confessio Catholica of 1561 should anchor Magyar Calvinism to the strictest Genevan doctrine. The tide spread eastward into Transylvania and but for the election of Stephen Báthory, the province might have been permanently won to the new faith. From this time Catholicism, Lutheranism, Calvinism and Unitarianism were all recognized in Transylvania. Here and in many other parts of Hungary there obtained a localized version of *cujus regio, ejus religio*. If a man did not like the religion practised in his district, he could freely move to another where the local magnates allowed a more congenial worship. The period of persecution in the Habsburg areas under Emperor Rudolph II (1576–1612) did not substantially alter the balance in Hungary. To our own times about a fifth of the population remained Calvinist, while the Lutheran minority (around 6 per cent) was largely limited to those of German and Slovak stock.

134 King Sigismund II Augustus (reigned 1548–72) and the Pope in coalition: engraving from Stanislaw Orzechowski's *Quincunx*, 1564, an argument for such an alliance in a sadly divided country. The legend reads, 'Whichever side you offended, you would break up the structure of the kingdom.' In the next year the Jesuits arrived in Poland

135 Stephen I Báthory followed the brief Valois interval, and his reign (1575–86) saw the Polish state at its zenith

The impact and social forms of Calvinism were diversely conditioned by these backgrounds. It trained men to operate in small and disciplined groups, which in their censorious superiority often show sectarian features. On the other hand, its sense of social discipline, its sober ethical atmosphere, its reassuring background in bourgeois Geneva made it infinitely more viable within conservative societies than the sects had been. In the absence of formidable opposition, it could readily gravitate from local to governmental power; it could even become the directing influence in a State. On the other hand, despite the great Calvinist or quasi-Calvinist financiers of seventeenth-century Europe, Calvinism cannot accurately be described as a movement dominated by big business interests. Everywhere it developed a considerable appeal for small tradesmen and craftsmen. The English Puritan armies were far from consisting solely of officers. The strength of strict Dutch Calvinism lay in the lesser citizens, while the regent class proved overwhelmingly liberal and Arminian.

Nowadays no one has a kind word for Max Weber's thesis that Calvinism created a new 'dedicated' capitalist outlook, the 'worldly asceticism' of modern business. It seems indeed difficult to construct any defence of this specious theory, which was given a new lease of life—yet very little more bone and sinew—by R. H. Tawney's work *Religion and the Rise of Capitalism*. Almost every feature of the sixteenth-century business world, including double-entry bookkeeping, had already existed in late medieval Europe. The Fuggers and most of the Augsburg bankers remained Catholics at the Reformation, while Europe's other chief centres of high finance —Antwerp, Lyons, Genoa, Venice—lay in Catholic countries. Again, the ideal of the hard-working and methodical life was preached by seventeenth-century Jesuits and Jansenists as well as by their Puritan contemporaries. On the whole, Calvinism fought the practices of unfettered capitalism more consistently than did any other of the Christian churches. Calvin himself placed even the banker under demands of the Sermon on the Mount, and he regarded the charging of interest as a dubious activity for a Christian. In his view, interest should never be taken from the poor. From the wealthy, lenders might take moderate interest as a fair share in the profit which their loans had made possible. Yet should a borrower lose capital or profit through no fault of his own, the Christian lender must not claim interest; indeed, he should not even press for the immediate repayment of the lost capital. With a striking uniformity these strict principles were maintained by the leading Calvinist theologians of succeeding generations. Moreover, the various Reformed churches strove to maintain them in the daily practice of their members: the English Puritans in particular upheld the strict and unworldly principles they had inherited from Latimer and other early Protestant moralists. Such principles were still being enunciated in all their severity by Richard Baxter at the Restoration.

The collapse of the Weber thesis does not necessarily entail a total severance between the religious and the economic history of this age. An example of more sophisticated reconsideration may be seen in Professor Trevor-Roper's recent analysis of the background, methods and outlook of the great Protestant financiers of the seventeenth century. The ingenuity of men like de Geer, Rambouillet, d'Herwarth and de Witte supported not only Christian IV, Richelieu and Gustavus Adolphus but even their adversaries, the Austrian and Spanish Habsburgs. Their history does not, it is true, tend to rehabilitate Weber. These financiers were nominal rather than devout Calvinists, their ways of life quite unmarked by any spirit of asceticism. The noticeable common factor of their backgrounds is not Calvinism at all, but rather the big business of Antwerp, and to a lesser extent that of the Liége district. Though several passed as Dutchmen, they or their fathers were immigrants not merely into the various countries where they operated, but first into the northern Netherlands. They were in fact children of the great emigration from the declining southern Netherlands during the last quarter of the sixteenth century, seeds of that *diaspora* from which the prosperity of the Dutch Republic so largely sprang. Trevor-Roper suggests that, if we seek to define the effects of religion upon business, we should turn to examine the action of the expelling Catholic powers, which so persistently forced critical and anticlerical townsmen into the arms of heresy and then drove them out to seek their fortunes elsewhere. Unlike the more tolerant Catholicism of the Middle Ages, that of the Counter Reformation monarchies had little room for city republics, hitherto the chief pillars of European commerce, industry and finance. Though extending favours to a few court-financiers and monopolists, the rulers of Spain, the southern Netherlands and Italy (except Venice, which understandably rejected these habits) expelled their business classes or discouraged them to the point of emigration. From the economic viewpoint, Catholic Europe thus tended to emasculate itself and to transfer power to the Protestant North and, at least until Louis XIV began persecuting, to France. More purely economic forces also promoted the original emigration from Antwerp, and the huge picture of course needs further definition. Yet the present writer finds this analysis far more convincing than those arising from the doctrinaire prejudices of Weber and his school.

On any showing, the political importance of Calvinism immensely exceeded its economic importance. However illiberal, Geneva was not politically sterile like illiberal Spain. Calvinism was not merely a discipline but a self-discipline. It could hence build communities capable of self-government, the basis of which lies in disciplined minds, not in political mechanisms. Identified from the first with city states and republican virtues, it found its political enemies where it found its religious enemies: in the great Catholic and autocratic monarchies of Europe. In many places it speedily linked with the emergent forces of nationalism and regionalism, and everywhere it showed the steely qualities of a fighting resistance-creed. Moreover, it believed in committees, in the rule of law, in constitutional organs. However little the restrictive polity of Calvin's Geneva may have seemed to prognosticate such a development, this was fated to become the creed of men who cared passionately for certain concepts of national and civic freedom. These men Calvinism helped to invest with a hardness and an independence lacking in the prince-worshippers of Luther's day. From the stifling parade-grounds of presbytery and synod, Sea Beggar and Huguenot, Puritan and Covenanter marched out to battlefields where at least some of the great issues of human freedom lay at stake.

136 The Marian burning at Oxford of Ridley and Latimer, Bishops of London and Worcester, 1555: from John Foxe's *Actes and Monuments*, 1563. Top right, Cranmer awaits his turn

PURITANISM AND ANGLICANISM

In world history as seen from the vantage-point of our own day, the story of Calvinism in England assumes a unique significance. English Puritanism gave a cutting edge to the forces which shaped parliamentary, legal and religious liberties as since understood throughout the English-speaking world. Overseas it led directly to experiments which could never have progressed far amid the spiritual and cultural multilateralism of the home country. One of its greatest achievements was the building of a series of genuinely Puritan societies in New England. To our generation this second outcome may well seem at least as important as the first, since New England, enlivened also by freer sectarian groups, powerfully imbued westward-spreading American society with mental traits still plainly discernible today. The 'American Gothic', the moralizing outlook, the black-and-white judgements were not only preserved in religious *milieux* but transferred to secular problems by minds retaining little conscious theological content. In America the Puritan sense of human corruption persisted as a counterbalance against the vapid idealization of human nature which eighteenth-century fashion superimposed on the Founding Fathers. Again, in this transatlantic society the English Puritan heritage received powerful reinforcement from the parallel Calvinist traditions of Scotland and Ulster, areas constrained by economic poverty to export their men and consequently their ideas. All in all, 'Anglo-Saxon' Puritanism became by far the lustiest child of Geneva and Zürich.

The advent of Calvinism to England began in the days of Henry VIII, who unintentionally prepared the way by giving the vernacular Bible to the people. With an equal inadvertence, the religious reaction of Henry's later years drove out several important English exiles and brought them into close contact with the Swiss Reformation. The most prominent of these men was John Hooper—often called the 'father of English Puritanism'—who lived at Zürich with Bullinger and associated with Calvinist zealots like the Polish exile John à Lasco. Hooper then returned to propagate 'advanced' views in the England of Edward VI. Here he received strong support from John Knox, and from 1549 to 1553 the pair exercised an influence greater than Cranmer's upon the religious policy of the opportunist government headed by John Dudley, Duke of Northumberland. During these same years thousands of continental refugees entered England, many of them from the areas oppressed by the Interim of Augsburg. Several, including Bucer and Peter Martyr, held prominent positions in both universities, while at the Austin Friars in the heart of London Cranmer freely permitted the immigrants to organize a Reformed Church outside English episcopal control. The overwhelming majority of these settlers looked not to Wittenberg but to Geneva, Zürich and Strassburg. Even among the moderate English theologians a corresponding shift of emphasis is clearly observable. About 1546 Cranmer and his chief adviser Ridley had already arrived by independent study of the Fathers at eucharistic views similar to those of Bucer. Their Forty-two Articles of 1552 showed some Calvinist influences and in the matter of predestination maintained the Genevan orthodoxy. Cranmer's second Prayer Book, though in no sense modelled upon the Zwinglian or Calvinist rites, nevertheless followed the trend to the extent of making its communion service predominantly one of commemoration.

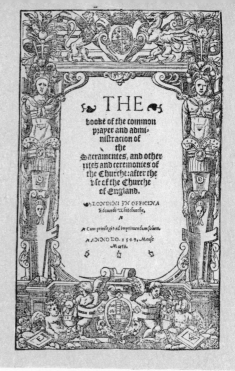

137, 138 The Geneva or 'Breeches' Bible, 1560, so called due to the Puritan thoroughness with which the first sinners are made to cover themselves in Genesis 3:7: title-page; *(right)* the title-page of Cranmer's first and more conservative Book of Common Prayer (1549)

Scarcely had this Prayer Book and the Articles been set forth, when the death of King Edward and the Catholic reaction under Queen Mary interrupted the experiment in State-Protestantism. About 800 of the leading English Protestants, now driven into exile, found themselves coolly received, even repulsed, by the cautious Lutheran communities. The latter not only disagreed with their eucharistic doctrines but also feared that their violently anti-Spanish attitudes (provoked by the unpopular union between Mary and Philip II) would endanger the current policies of compromise with the Habsburgs. Hence the chief settlements of English refugees were established at Strassburg, Zürich and Geneva, though those at Frankfurt-am-Main and at Emden also showed vitality. About a quarter of the exiles were for some time resident in Geneva, where their leaders produced a voluminous literature of controversy,

183

together with the long-popular metrical psalms and that Geneva Version of the English Bible, so frequently republished in Elizabethan England. At Frankfurt there occurred bitter quarrels between those who wanted to retain 'the face of an English church'—in particular to use the second Prayer Book—and the whole-hearted advocates of Calvinism headed by Knox and William Whittingham. And while the Prayer Book men succeeded in getting Knox driven out of Frankfurt, they themselves also revered Calvin and appealed to his authority. On Mary's death they hastily returned to England, headed by Jewel and Cox built up a pressure-group in the House of Commons, and in the crucial Parliament of 1559 struck a bargain with the cautious and conservatively-minded young Elizabeth. She adopted the second Prayer Book with certain modifications, while they accepted office in a national Church organized on the old basis of episcopacy, with its medieval courts and legal structure little altered.

Upon the subsequent return of the disappointed Genevan group, the historic dichotomy within the Anglican Church became ever more clearly apparent. Yet the key to the understanding of Elizabethan and Jacobean religion lies in the internality of the dispute and in the slightness of its theological content. Until the reign of Charles I, separatist movements, even movements towards Presbyterian church government, formed but a tiny fraction of the great volume of English Calvinist Puritanism. While the latter created a restive party within the Anglican Church, it nevertheless remained an integral element, indeed the most active and dominant element. Until the closing years of Elizabeth's reign it is not easy to isolate and define any vital spirituality or any intellectual movement within Anglicanism which was not deeply impregnated by Calvinism. Even as Archbishop Whitgift attempted to discipline scrupulous objectors to the surplice, the sign of the cross and the marriage-ring, he himself never strayed far from Genevan orthodoxy when it came to the essential doctrines. For five years his predecessor Grindal had stood suspended from jurisdictional functions for refusing to suppress the 'prophesyings' or scriptural conferences held by the Puritan clergy. Meanwhile the University of Cambridge poured into the Anglican

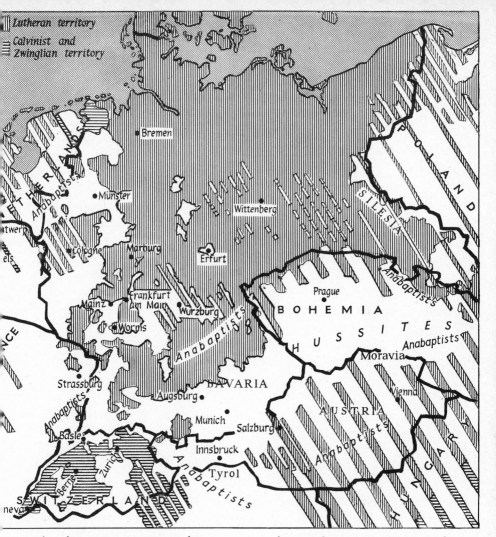

Bremen

NETHERLANDS

Anabaptists

Antwerp

Münster

Wittenberg

POLAND

SILESIA

Cologne

Marburg

Erfurt

Mainz

Frankfurt am Main

Würzburg

Prague

BOHEMIA

HUSSITES

Anabaptists

Worms

Anabaptists

Moravia

Anabaptists

FRANCE

Strassburg

BAVARIA

Augsburg

Vienna

Anabaptists

Basle

Munich

Salzburg

AUSTRIA

Zürich

Innsbruck

Anabaptists

Berne

Tyrol

HUNGARY

SWITZERLAND

Geneva

139 The religious situation in central Europe *c.* 1550, showing the approximate extent of the revolt from Rome

ministry a stream of graduates trained in the same Calvinist principles. In the Commons Puritan activists urged the Queen toward more decisively Protestant policies; some of them even hankered after the Presbyterian system. In many towns and districts, the godly magistrates appointed lecturers and chaplains of their own stamp, striving to mould their local environments into little Genevas.

Intelligibly enough, some hard things have been said of the English Puritans; it was doubtless well that bounds should have been set to tendencies otherwise likely to have marred some of the greatest intellectual and spiritual achievements of Englishmen. On the other hand, it must not be forgotten that Milton and Cromwell and Bunyan were also sons of the Puritan tradition.

During the last years of Elizabeth's reign Calvinist orthodoxy began to encounter an opposition weightier than the mere official demand for compliance with the Prayer Book. Anglicanism had never lost the potentiality to become something more complex than a medieval body inhabited by a Calvinist spirit. Many of the concepts of a *via media* national Church had been familiar to Englishmen since the 'thirties, a time when Calvin was almost unknown in England. Many Englishmen were attracted by the liberal and latitudinarian aspects of the theologies of Erasmus, Bucer and Melanchthon. In Cranmer's Prayer Books there were strong Catholic and Lutheran elements: these the Elizabethan Prayer Book retained, while implicitly allowing a latitude of eucharistic belief. Anglicanism thus had some prepared exits from the straight and narrow Genevan highway. Though nearly all Elizabeth's earliest bishops came from the ranks of the Marian exiles, this was not true of her first primate Matthew Parker, tolerant in doctrine, almost Erasmian, by personal taste an antiquary rather than a theologian. As the decades passed there came a weakening of the ties which bound Elizabeth's senior clergy to the Swiss Reformed religion, and when adequate alternative concepts began to present themselves they did not fail to attract support.

This relaxation became noticeable in the mid-nineties. In 1594 Richard Hooker published the first four books of his *Laws of Ecclesiastical Polity*, the famous fifth book following three years later. In most respects this remarkable *apologia* cannot be claimed as a forerunner of 'high' churchmanship. Hooker denied, for example, the necessity of episcopal ordination, while like Cranmer (and unlike the Catholics and the Lutherans) he believed that the sacramental presence was partaken by the communicant through faith, and not localized in the bread and wine. On the other hand, he administered

some hard blows to the extremer Puritans. He denied the fundamentalism which had led the latter to regard the Bible as a rigid,
immutable and consistent book of rules. He urged that even the
Scriptures are subservient to the natural law, the supreme reason by
which God governs the universe and the hearts of men. The Church
he regards as a developing and organic institution, the Church of
England as a reformed continuity from the medieval Church.
During these same years the rigours of Cambridge theology came
to be tempered by the anti-predestinarian doctrines which Jacobus
Arminius, then at Amsterdam, was working out in opposition to
William Perkins, the greatest of the Cambridge Calvinists. This
particular controversy did not come to a head until 1598, but already
in 1595-6 the Cambridge professor Peter Baro taught that Christ
died for all men and that human free will played a part in the process
of salvation. As early as April 1595 his aggressive pupil William
Barrett stunned Cambridge by a full-blooded attack on Calvin and
was forced to recant in the university church. While the aged
Archbishop Whitgift took the side of Calvinist authority, he soon
afterwards relinquished leadership of the Anglican Church to
Richard Bancroft, bishop of London, who did not hesitate to show
his approval of Baro's doctrines. By the last years of the century the
stage was prepared both in England and in the northern Netherlands
for an open confrontation between Calvinism and Arminianism, a
confrontation to be exploited in both countries by major political
forces. Hence in countries where the Catholic Counter Reformation
could not penetrate, the triumphant march of Calvinism was now
being arrested by forces quite different, by doctrines still distinctly
Protestant, yet based on a vision broader and potentially more
humane. That this happened within the two most economically,
socially and intellectually 'progressive' nations of Europe can be
numbered among the portents of a new age of religious history.

X SOME CONTEXTS AND SEQUELS

In their preoccupation with secular results modern intellectuals sometimes overlook the most direct and obvious outcome of Protestantism and radicalism: the formation of churches and sects, so many of which have survived, amid mutations and rebirths, into our own age. Through these institutions the message of the Reformers has permeated the lives of many millions of men and women throughout successive generations. The most demonstrable effect of the Reformation lies in the propagation among these millions of an enlarged and less man-shaped concept of God, one divested of side-cults, one aiming to restore primitive Christianity by reference to the documents, one entailing fresh human responses, new codes of worship and conduct. Despite internal dissensions, the great mass of the movement continued to revolve around the justificatory issue raised by Luther during the early days of his revolt. In the long run this strictly religious issue weighed more heavily than did those concerning mere ecclesiastical reform. To put the matter bluntly, Luther made far deeper marks than did Erasmus upon the religious, social and political configuration of Europe. Luther's movement and its Calvinist extension had palpable results through functioning churches and sects. In contrast the influence of Erasmus soon became diffused not only between Catholic and Protestant reformers but within a host of secular movements, literary, scholarly, scientific, so that it lost any capacity for independent or institutional action. Protestantism used humanist critical techniques for its own ends somewhat as it used the medieval heresies and the *devotio moderna*, but its debts necessarily remained limited, because its theology and its philosophy of man were diametrically opposed to those of humanism.

As the formative stages of the Reformation were involved with Christian humanism, so its developed stages became involved with the Counter Reformation, which so swiftly proceeded to diminish the empire of Protestantism. Organized Catholic reform had been operating on a limited scale with Ximenes and other prelates around the turn of the century. Even as Luther presented his account, it was already revitalizing Italian religious houses and founding new orders. It did not begin as a *Counter* Reformation, and many years later St Ignatius Loyola established his Society without at first clearly envisaging its task as an assault upon European heresies. There would assuredly have occurred a Catholic Reformation had Protestantism never developed, but we cannot profitably conjecture the type or degree of success it would in that event have attained, since it had not advanced far when its programme became dominated by the massive crisis facing the whole Catholic Church. In other words, the work of Loyola and Canisius cannot be assessed save in the context of a world shaken to its foundations by Luther and Calvin.

To a striking degree the heroic achievements of the Counter Reformation, those which modified the religious map of Europe, were accomplished by the Society of Jesus, which not only checked the further spread of Protestantism but greatly weakened its hold upon southern central Europe and Poland, the areas where it stood least securely established. In passing, we should not fail to observe that both movements failed to advance farther eastward still; the more vital yet more divided West hence left so much of the Slavonic world looking to Orthodox Christianity and ultimately to Moscow, 'the third Rome'. Meanwhile the significance of the Council of Trent extended far beyond its ostensible reforms. Its direct contribution lay chiefly in its attack upon the old problem of clerical education, especially in its provision of a seminary in each diocese. Yet even more important was its indirect rôle as the Council to end Councils, as the Council which laid the unquiet ghost of Conciliarism and delivered the Church to a long era of papal monarchy. And even while the new Catholicism geographically restricted the Protestant Reformation, the latter wrought its indirect revenge by setting mental bounds to the former. While Protestantism provoked no little heroism and endeavour in its opponents, it also provoked in them those habits of doctrinaire conservatism which passed far outside the religious field and ended by limiting the appeal of Rome.

That the mighty opposites preserved their integrities at an enormous price in human suffering, one comes to realize during any detailed study of the French Wars of Religion or the Thirty Years War. Nevertheless only a part of the blame for these disasters, so largely political in origin, should be laid at the door of religious bigotry, while on the credit side it may at least be urged that the freedom and national consciousness of Holland, Switzerland, England and Scotland bear heavy debts towards the religious changes of the sixteenth century. Certainly these changes helped to create that magnificent diversification of European culture which marked the succeeding age. Had they not occurred, it is hard to imagine how anything like the world of Milton, Rembrandt, Newton and Bach could have come to birth alongside the baroque splendours of the Catholic South. The cultural impacts of Protestantism were sometimes direct, as with the German musical tradition, sometimes oblique, as with Rembrandt: in both cases they must be recognized as wholly essential to the result.

SECULARIZATION AND ITS EFFECTS

We have suggested that the extra-religious effects of the Reformation have been exaggerated by those who sought to invert Marxist priorities and to credit Protestantism with the paternity of modern western capitalism. We might claim that the real sins of Protestant society lay in the reverse process, in the tendency to exclude business practice from the purview of the religious world. It nevertheless remains questionable whether Catholic industrial societies have integrated the two with any greater success. For the reasons we have mentioned, this whole approach seems to have proved a *cul de sac* of historiography and if we seek the economic effects of the Reformation we are more likely to find them in material fact rather than in social psychology. Especially should we examine the widespread transfer of church lands to lay or state ownership, since in no country have the precise implications of this territorial revolution been so fully investigated as the sources will allow. Both its immediate and its remoter sequels proved far from uniform.

In Sweden Gustavus Vasa deprived the Church of all its landed properties, offering the dubious argument that since his predecessors had given them he had the right to recover them. The proportion of land held by the crown increased during his reign from 5·5 per cent to 28 per cent: that of the Church fell from 21 per cent to nil, while the shares of the nobility and the peasant farmers did not significantly alter. Afterwards, especially during the seventeenth century, crown lands were alienated on a large scale to the nobility, though after 1680 Charles XI recovered a substantial part of the losses. None of these changes materially diminished the almost unique degree of freedom and privilege enjoyed by the Swedish peasantry.

In both Brandenburg and Prussia both the prior conditions and the outcome proved different. Here the Hohenzollern rulers seized the monastic lands, yet were forced by lack of money to sell or pawn a large part of them to noblemen. In both these territories, as also in Pomerania, the Reformation did not, as commonly supposed, help to institute autocracy. In fact it was followed by the apotheosis of a nobility now passionately interested in agricultural profits and well able to translate its economic triumph into political power. Trampling down both the peasantry and the towns, the Junkers also controlled their princes through the Estates and through their monopoly of administrative offices. Only a century later, amid the new conditions succeeding the Thirty Years War, did the Hohenzollern princes centralize administration and achieve a true partnership with the Junker class. And while the secularization of monastic estates may well have hastened the already evident decline of the peasantry, an even more striking growth of serfdom occurred in Poland. Yet there the ecclesiastical landlords—at all times notoriously rich and grasping—successfully defended their lands and privileges, and with no perceptible benefit to the peasants.

Professor Carsten's recent studies of the German princes and their Estates have thrown further light upon similar aspects of the Reformation in Württemberg, Hesse, Albertine Saxony and other Protestant states. In all these lands the greater part of the former monastic revenue was devoted to public purposes, including education and charity. In Hesse about 40 per cent went to the State;

in the rest a very much smaller proportion. Everywhere the Estates took pains to ensure that the prince made little profit and in each case the price-rise within a few years forced the prince back to his former financial dependence upon the Estates. In short, German princely power did not much benefit from the Reformation, which failed to overthrow the political and social equilibrium. The Estates gained more influence than the rulers and in these territories they later constituted themselves the real defenders of orthodox Lutheranism. Except in Catholic Bavaria, their position waxed stronger throughout the sixteenth century; where a decline occurred, it belonged to a later age and did not spring from this process of secularization.

In England the initial results of the monastic dissolution bore some resemblance to those in north-eastern Germany. Involved in costly warfare with France and Scotland, Henry VIII sold off about two-thirds of his newly-acquired monastic lands. Bought freely by men of both Catholic and Protestant leanings, these lands multiplied the existent gentry, most of all by affording opportunities to younger sons hitherto debarred from inheriting land by the principle of primogeniture. This redistribution does not appear notably to have changed the tenor and practices of English landlordism; certainly there occurred no revival of serfdom. On the other hand the numerical growth and collective enrichment of the gentry is not without reason accounted one of the factors underlying the victories won by the House of Commons over the Stuart Kings. Meanwhile the English Church lost about half its landed possessions, while in the House of Lords the disappearance of the major abbots left the lay peers with a majority of seats.

In all Protestant countries, the numbers, wealth and political influence of the clergy underwent drastic reduction. While many of their former functions were taken over by the growing classes of literate laymen, the social influence of the clergy cannot be supposed to have fallen proportionately with their numbers, for they became a more select body with higher educational standards and an enhanced moral prestige. Again, the influence of a married clergy—and of clerical families in general—constituted a new and often valuable element, especially in the rural society of Protestant countries. While the shifting situation of the churches produced some important social effects, the more purely economic results of secularization have probably been overestimated. The process seems slightly to have intensified some economic tendencies without creating new ones; indeed, to an overwhelming extent both the economic and the political phenomena of the Reformation period sprang from plain economic and political causes. Charities and good works did not noticeably decline in the face of solifidianism, though they were channelled to a lesser degree through the churches. And while in later centuries some Lutherans made ovine subjects in Brandenburg-Prussia, autocracy also flourished in Catholic countries, while other Lutherans developed the constitutional monarchies of Scandinavia. As already observed, Calvinism became a directive force of the revolts and nationalist movements which united with well-marked geographical and economic differentials to give the Atlantic, North Sea and Baltic regions a dynamic greater than that of the Mediterranean lands. The Reformation helped in that swing of the balance whereby north-western Europe became more socially and scientifically creative than the other regions. On the morrow of its failure to dominate eastern Europe and enter Russia, Protestantism in all its forms crossed the Atlantic. Its victories on the European seaboard hence led to the rise of a North American society so heavily permeated by Protestant concepts as at last to alter the local ethos of Catholicism itself. Here all the religions of Europe came to confront each other in an atmosphere of self-conscious liberalism, free from dynastic manipulation by Habsburg and Bourbon, free ultimately from the grip of Anglican and Calvinist orthodoxies. Nowhere has the Reformation exerted more powerful and far-reaching influences; nowhere do they remain so pregnant for the future of humanity.

THE SCIENTIFIC REVOLUTION

Even as this overseas expansion occurred, the rise of natural philosophy culminated in the Newtonian universe and thence in rationalism and the Enlightenment. Many historians of Protestantism have naturally sought to investigate its relations with the scientific revolution from Copernicus to Newton, but the diversity of their findings would again suggest the dangers of simple formulae. The first Reformers proved oblivious enough to the new hypotheses: both Luther and Calvin fondly imagined they could demolish Copernicus by quoting the Old Testament. In turn we find Puritanism working in conjunction with a huge variety of cultural influences old and new, yet in general tending to lack disinterested curiosity towards problems outside the religious and social spheres. And while the Inquisition and the Index continued to hamper some branches of science long after Protestant theologians had ceased to do so, many natural philosophers, including Jesuits, Jansenists and even Spaniards, contrived to work in Catholic countries and to take their places in the common advance. Despite the local obstructions, Galileo in particular built some vital stretches of the great highway.

It proved nevertheless of vital importance that Protestant ecclesiasticism failed to grasp the sceptre of the medieval Church. Within the Protestant North there occurred no general apotheosis of Thomism and the slow decline of reverence towards Aristotle was soon followed by a weakening of Protestant biblical fundamentalism. There during the seventeenth century experimental and observational philosophy could the more readily escape ecclesiastical controls. Nevertheless in Lutheran Germany a knowledge of Aristotelian philosophy remained in that period a hallmark of the cultured man. Here Melanchthon's scholastic philosophy survived the collapse of his theology. Lutheranism had spoken with two voices and Luther's own attack upon Aristotle formed only one of the many preliminaries to the demolition of Aristotelian cosmology. Yet with much more significance Calvin liquidated the hierarchies of angels which had presided over the Christian cosmos since the time of the Pseudo-Dionysius; he asserted that God governed the universe directly and not mediately through these agents, in fact that God had predetermined all events from the beginning of time. This withdrawal from anthropomorphic notions towards a universe under a single law at least led men in the general direction of the great Newtonian machine. Some of Calvin's successors among the

194

English Puritans developed the theory of cosmic absolutism to the point of urging that God is bound by his own ordinances, that he cannot do what is contrary to the Law of Nature. And to cite a less familiar link, it has been shown how closely the Anti-Trinitarian ideas of Servetus were related to his rejection of Aristotelian cosmology and even to his prophetic theory of the lesser circulation of the blood.

RELIGIOUS TOLERATION AND SECULARISM

During the century 1550–1650 there seems on balance little to choose between Catholic and Protestant Europe in the matter of religious toleration. If the former contained intransigent Spain, it could also boast the two countries, France and Poland, where Catholic governments attempted prolonged essays in legalized tolerance. Likewise, despite the arrogance of many Protestant theologians and the stiff orthodoxies of Wittenberg and Geneva, there had always been growth-points for liberalism in the Protestant tree: early Luther on Christian liberty, Philip Melanchthon's adiaphorism and ecumenism, the eirenic labours of Bucer, the tentative Cranmer, seeing good in almost everyone except the Anabaptists. As the Reformation advanced there arose a succession of downright antagonists of religious persecution: Sebastian Castellio (d. 1563), Mino Celsi, William Turner, Jacobus Acontius, Alberico Gentili, John Foxe, Edwin Sandys and a number of others who are rightly given places among the founding fathers of religious liberalism. These men, like the Catholic *Politiques* and the Huguenot tolerationists in France, stood to some extent in the humanist tradition, and rationalists once delighted to depict them as torch-bearers of Classical enlightenment amid the darkness of Christianity. In actual fact their writings afford extremely little ground for this wishful simplification. They were Christians whose objections to juridical persecution by Church and State sprang largely from their study of the Gospels and from the resultant concept of a Christianity based on persuasion and love. Meanwhile within the political world, especially in England, the persecution of Catholics by Protestant governments was based on fear of Spain and of counter-revolution rather than on religious principles, and it tended to be abandoned or inefficiently exercised during periods of relative security. Outside the sphere of the only Church which claimed universal and exclusive authority, political opportunism soon displaced true religious persecution. Amid muddled politico-religious hatreds, the concept of heresy as a punishable offence slowly withered. More broadly, the national, confessional and sectarian Churches failed to establish that grip upon intellectual life and public opinion attained by the medieval Church or, throughout half the continent, by the Church of the Counter Reformation.

From about the middle of the sixteenth century even northern Europe saw a secularizing of mental interests, and this not only among the growing host of literate laymen but also among the educated clergy. The process can readily be illustrated by a mass-study of published works or by reference to private library catalogues, wills and inventories. Erasmian humanism should doubtless be regarded as an important tributary to this broad stream, but the stream soon became too voluminous and complex to remain susceptible of this facile title. Montaigne, Shakespeare, Kepler, Bacon and Descartes cannot helpfully be labelled as Erasmians; they were far more deeply secular in their interests than Erasmus (who spent so much of his life editing the Fathers!) and they gave the intellectual life of Europe dimensions beyond those of early sixteenth-century humanism, whether Christian or non-Christian. This new and formidable development, for which our books have no accepted title, came to full stature alongside the Reformation and educated Christian believers found themselves increasingly compelled to adjust themselves to its implications. Many, in Sir Thomas Browne's famous metaphor, found themselves becoming amphibians and consciously swimming in more than one intellectual element. Like the Italians of the High Renaissance, yet in a deeper and subtler sense, they lived compartmented lives, and these now bore little relation to Lutheran, Calvinist or Jesuit ideals. Hence the religious leaders, having brushed aside the superficial theology of Erasmus, came up against opposition far more formidable. They found themselves in a world which had made itself far more independent of

Christian controls than the world of the later Middle Ages. The churches found this secular spirit all the more difficult to manage because it was seldom defiantly anti-Christian, because its humanism was not merely Erasmian humanism, because it could now produce ideas more fascinating to intelligent men than the old subtleties of theology. From this point we need to appraise intellectual and religious history in terms of appeal rather than in terms of mortal combat or judicial compulsion.

THE REFORMATION IN RECENT TIMES

It would clearly seem misleading to conclude our survey at the points where secularism, science and rationalism began so profoundly to modify the results of the Protestant Reformation. Alongside and after these developments arose some very different portents: the diversification and liberalizing of both Anglicanism and Lutheranism; the continued proliferation of sects and evangelical movements; the rise of Methodism, with its strong debt to Luther; several distinguished exponents of religious sensibility from William Law to Friedrich Schleiermacher. These neo-Reformation tendencies culminated in the revival of Protestant Christianity which marked the nineteenth century. The positive effects of the Reformation should always be assessed with due regard to this last astonishing period of enrichment and expansion, which at once inherited and superseded Reformation, rationalism and pietism alike. Kierkegaard and some of his contemporaries were the executors of Luther and the step-fathers of the Luther-Renaissance still in progress. The Reformers and radicals of the sixteenth century had lineal successors in the Protestant thinkers, missionaries, revivalists and organizers of the nineteenth, when the Christian faith, so far from suffering further rout at the hands of scientific enlightenment, staged some of the greatest geographical and intellectual advances in its whole history. Despite their enormous losses and failures, both Protestantism and Catholicism were stronger throughout the world in 1914 than they had been in 1815.

The nineteenth century applied great intellects and sophisticated techniques to the problems which had faced Erasmus, Luther and

Calvin; moreover it applied them to the problems besetting Christianity in its recent philosophical and scientific contexts. It was the age not only of Schleiermacher and Kierkegaard, but of Baur, Ritschl, Troeltsch, Harnack, Westcott and Hort. By any criteria of intellectual achievement, these historical and theological revaluations of Christianity deserve a place among the more brilliant achievements of the last century. Such thinking could not have grown except upon the thought of the original Protestant Reformation, but it was far less fettered to antique concepts or to the dead hand of repressive legalism. In dwelling unduly upon its contradictory trends we can miss its collective achievement: the raising of Christian problems to new planes of knowledge and analysis. Collectively these men created a vast new stock-in-trade of ideas and significant questions in large measure shared by serious Christian thought since their time; somewhat paradoxically they and their great successors of the present century have led the various denominations into conference rather than into division. They dwarfed the inter-denominational squabbles of Protestant ecclesiasticism and restored Christianity to its rightful place in the exchanges of thoughtful and educated men. Herein lay the triumph of an age in which free discussion occurred on a scale hitherto quite unknown in Christian history. In our own century still more of the intellectual background which restricted the early Reformed and Counter Reformers has been jettisoned. The issues raised by Luther have still, no doubt, a deep relevance for many of the generation which is finding Teilhard de Chardin relevant. Yet one has only to compare the approaches of the two in order to perceive that Luther's message now embraces a diminished proportion of the world of religious thought—a world ever further enlarged by the advance of the physical sciences, of history, biblical criticism, sociology and psychology. The era of dialogue has followed the era of radical controversy; time and free criticism have tended to eliminate the wilder and the flimsier hypotheses. At a price—and here nothing is gained save at a price—Protestantism has begun to make its way through a measure of synthesis towards new visions of spiritual unity. Indeed, these and other recent experiences suggest that Christianity is less threatened by free doctrinal speculation than by heresy-hunting on the one hand, and by mindless indifference on the other.

Not alone in theology and history did the nineteenth century prove itself heir to the sixteenth. It did so in the fecundity of its new missionary organizations and techniques; again in its gradual over-throw of *laissez faire* complacency and its ultimate creation of a social Christianity which appreciates the interdependence of body and soul. Even amid the uprooting and transplanting of peoples, Christian belief and organization contrived to flourish. In the days of President Madison it would not have been easy to foresee the vast population-growth of the United States. But it would have been far more hazardous to conjecture that a century-and-a-half later some 60 per cent of this population would still be in Church member-ship: that the few original Catholics would by then have multiplied to 32 millions; that among the 57 million Protestants there would be numbered some 18 million Baptists, $11\frac{1}{2}$ million Methodists, 7 million Lutherans, $3\frac{1}{2}$ million Presbyterians, $2\frac{1}{2}$ million Episco-palians. We Europeans affect to despise statistics. Yet do not these figures form a crushing answer to historians who believe the Reformation relatively unimportant? Do they not also serve to correct the notion, so often repeated by European journalists, novelists and other creatures of vogue, that the Christian churches are empty?

Measured in terms of reunion, the nineteenth century seemed at the time a period of continuing loss, but it now appears in fact to have been laying the basis for those tasks of our own century: the forging of institutional unions between Protestant churches and the establishment of practical co-operation between the Protestant and the Catholic worlds. On the first issue, the most sober observers can now speak in optimistic terms. In South India, in Canada, in Central Africa and in Germany major unions have been achieved. At this moment of writing, further important unions are actually being negotiated in Britain, in Nigeria, Ghana, North India, Pakistan, Ceylon and Australia. Too often the ecumenical movements decided from above have been unduly slow in percolating to the congregational level. Yet one thing at least is clear. Those who earlier in our century dismissed Protestantism as infinitely fissiparous spoke too soon in the day. And even in relation to the harder task shared between Protestants and Catholics, there has at least occurred on both sides a change of spirit which would have shocked former generations and which even twenty years ago seemed to lie in some future century.

Since the events which our present essay relates, the history of the Christian religion has been so full of dramatic and unpredictable changes of course that it appears to contain forces capable of defeating the calculations of politicians, planners and historians. In a redemptive rationality controlling such forces the present writer profoundly wishes to believe, for he cannot see that self-reliant humanity has begun to purge itself of the universal taint of selfhood described by St Paul and by Luther. We have not yet reached the final curtain, yet thus far our performances as players might well make us shrink from desiring to be, in addition, sole authors of the divine comedy.

Readers wishing to pursue further these and similar topics will find an excellent starting-point in *The Oxford Dictionary of the Christian Church*, ed. F. L. Cross (1957).

ADIAPHORISM
(Greek *adiaphora*, 'things indifferent'). The principle that some commonly accepted doctrines and rituals cannot be proved essentials of the Faith, or binding upon Christians.

ALBIGENSES
The sect important in southern France from the eleventh to the early thirteenth centuries, when it was in large part extirpated by a lengthy 'crusade'. Its wholesale rejection of Catholic doctrines was based upon a dualism which regarded matter as evil.

ANTINOMIANISM
The belief that Christians are by grace set free from the need to observe moral laws.

ANTINOMY
One of a pair of mutually conflicting laws or sequences of thought, each of which possesses, or appears to possess, equal validity.

AVERROISM
The philosophy maintained by Siger of Brabant (d. *c.* 1282) and other anti-Thomist thinkers, who derived from Averroes (d. 1198), the Arab commentator on Aristotle. Averroism was notorious *inter alia* for the 'double truth', i.e. that one could deny, as a philosopher, conclusions one accepted as a theologian.

CATHARISTS
(Greek *katharos*, 'pure'). A term applied to various sects, especially to the ALBIGENSES (q.v.) and the parallel, contemporary movements in Germany and Italy.

ERASTIANISM
The theory that the State should direct and determine the affairs of the Church: derived from the name of the Swiss theologian Thomas Erastus (1524–83).

EVANGELICAL
The term applied to Lutheran religion, as opposed to 'Reformed' (i.e. Calvinist) beliefs. Since the eighteenth century it has also been applied to the 'Low Church' party of the Anglican Church, which likewise emphasizes personal conversion and salvation by faith.

IMPUTATION
Luther's doctrine that the superabundant merits of Christ are immediately imputed to those men justified by their faith; i.e. reckoned to their credit even though they lack personal righteousness. This contrasts with the Catholic doctrine whereby Christ's merits are *imparted* to the faithful and produce gradual inward amelioration.

NOMINALISM
The scholastic system of philosophy and theology called the *via moderna*, as

opposed to fourteenth-century Realism, called the *via antiqua*. From its leading practitioner, Nominalism has become almost synonymous with Occamism. The system is based on the belief that universals, or general abstract terms, are names or words only and have no realities or objective existences corresponding to them.

PANTHEISM
The belief that God and the universe are identical. The mystics, seeking union with God and the presence of God in nature, sometimes verged on this belief.

PELAGIANISM
The theological system named after Pelagius (a British monk of the fourth and fifth centuries), which claimed that a man can take the initial steps toward salvation by his own efforts, apart from the assistance of divine grace. See SYNERGISM.

SOLIFIDIANISM
The belief that a man is justified (i.e. put in a saving relationship with God) by faith alone, without good works.

SPIRITUALISM
The term nowadays widely applied to those stressing the mystical approach to religion, or the authentication of doctrine by inward experience.

SYNERGISM
The belief that in the act of conversion the human will can co-operate with divine grace. While propounding this belief, Melanchthon rebutted the charge of PELAGIANISM (q.v.) by insisting that the *primary* cause of such co-operation is the Holy Spirit.

TRANSUBSTANTIATION
The doctrine that the whole 'substance' (i.e. underlying permanent reality) of the bread and wine are changed at consecration into the whole 'substance' of the Body and Blood of Christ, only the 'accidents' (i.e. appearances) of the bread and wine remaining. Transubstantiation was defined as *de fide* by the Lateran Council of 1215 and by the Council of Trent.

UTRAQUISM
The Hussite doctrine that the laity were entitled, like the clergy, to receive communion under the species of wine as well as under that of bread (*sub utraque specie*).

READING-LIST OF WORKS IN ENGLISH

This list contains some of the books and articles used by the writer and thought likely to interest readers of the present book. Most of them are quite recent and many do not yet appear in the standard bibliographies. Places of publication appear only for books published outside the U.K.

GENERAL

Allen, J. W., *A History of Political Thought in the Sixteenth Century* (3rd edn., 1951)

Bainton, R. H., *The Reformation of the Sixteenth Century* (1953)

Bainton, R. H., *Studies on the Reformation*, Series Two (Boston, 1963)

Chadwick, O., *The Reformation* (1964)

Daniel-Rops, H., *The Protestant Reformation* (1961)

Elton, G. R., *Reformation Europe, 1517–1559* (1963)

Gelder, H. A. E. van, *The Two Reformations in the 16th Century* (trans. J. F. Finlay, The Hague, 1961)

Hill, C., 'Protestantism and the Rise of Capitalism' in *Essays in the Economic and Social History of Tudor and Stuart England in Honour of R. H. Tawney* (1961)

Holl, K., *The Cultural Significance of the Reformation* (New York, 1959)

Hughes, P., *The Reformation* (1957)

Hyma, A., *The Christian Renaissance* (1925)

Hyma, A., *Renaissance to Reformation* (Grand Rapids, 1951)

Lecler, J., *Toleration and the Reformation* (trans. T. L. Weston, 2 vols., 1960)

Mackinnon, J., *The Origins of the Reformation* (1939)

Mason, S. F., 'The Scientific Revolution and the Protestant Reformation' in *Annals of Science*, IX (1953), 64–87, 154–75 (on the same theme, see also the same writer in *Past and Present*, No. 3, and H. F. Kearney in *ibid.*, No. 28)

Mattingly, G., *The Defeat of the Spanish Armada* (1959)

New Cambridge Modern History, I, ed. G. R. Potter (1961); II, ed. G. R. Elton (1958)

Phillips, M. M., *Erasmus and the Northern Renaissance* (1949)

Smith, Preserved, *The Age of the Reformation* (New York, 1920)

Sykes, N., *The Crisis of the Reformation* (1938)

Trevor-Roper, H. R., 'Religion, the Reformation and Social Change' in *Historical Studies*, IV (1963), 18–44

Troeltsch, E., *The Social Teaching of the Christian Churches* (trans. O. Wyon, 1931)

Whale, J. S., *The Protestant Tradition* (1955)

Whitney, J. P., *The History of the Reformation* (1958)

SOURCES

Calvin, J., *Works* (Calvin Translation Society edn., Edinburgh, 1843–55)

Calvin, J., *Institutes of the Christian Religion* (trans. H. Beveridge, 1949)

Dillenberger, J., *Martin Luther, Selections from his Writings* (New York, 1961)

Gee, H., and Hardy, W. J., *Documents Illustrative of English Church History* (1896)

Hillerbrand, H. J., *The Reformation in its Own Words* (1964)

Kidd, B. J., *Documents Illustrative of the Continental Reformation* (1911)

Library of Christian Classics, XIV–XXV [edns. of works by the leading Reformers]

Luther's Works (Concordia Publishing House, St Louis, from 1955: 55 vols.)

Woolf, B. L., *Reformation Writings of Martin Luther* (1952)

LUTHER AND LUTHERANISM

Allen, J. W., 'The Political Conceptions of Luther' in *Tudor Studies Presented to A. F. Pollard*, ed. R. W. Seton-Watson (1924)

Atkinson, J. (ed.), *Luther: Early Theological Works* (Library of Christian Classics, XVI, 1962)

Atkinson, J., 'The Significance of Martin Luther' in *The Churchman*, LXXVIII (1964), 108–15

Bainton, R. H., *Here I Stand: A Life of Martin Luther* (1950)

Baron, H., 'Religion and Politics in the German Imperial Cities during the Reformation' in *English Historical Review*, LII (1937), 405–27, 614–33

Barraclough, G., *The Origins of Modern Germany* (1946, 1947)

Boehmer, H., *Road to Reformation* (trans. J. W. Doberstein and T. G. Tappert, Philadelphia, 1946)

Bornkamm, H., *Luther's World of Thought* (trans. M. H. Bertram, St Louis, 1958)

Carsten, H. L., *The Origins of Prussia* (1954)

Carsten, H. L., *Princes and Parliaments in Germany* (1959)

Dunkley, E. H., *The Reformation in Denmark* (1948)

Eells, H., *Martin Bucer* (New Haven, 1931)

Ettinghausen, W., 'Luther: Exegesis and Prose Style' in *German Studies presented to H. G. Fiedler* (1938), 174–86

Fife, R. H., *The Revolt of Martin Luther* (New York, 1957)

Green, V. H. H., *Luther and the Reformation* (1964)

Grimm, H. J., 'Social Forces in the German Reformation' in *Church History*, XXXI (1962), 3–13

Hildebrandt, F., *Melanchthon: Alien or Ally?* (1946)

Holborn, H., *A History of Modern Germany: the Reformation* (1965)

Lau, F., *Luther* (trans. R. H. Fischer, 1963)

Mackinnon, J., *Luther and the Reformation* (4 vols., 1925–30)

Pascal, R., *The Social Basis of the German Reformation* (1933)

Pelikan, J., *Luther the Expositor* [Companion Volume to the series, *Luther's Works*] (St Louis, 1959)

Pelikan, J., *From Luther to Kierkegaard* (St Louis, 1950, 1963)

Ranke, L. von, *History of the Reformation in Germany* (trans. S. Austin, 3 vols., 1845–7)

Ritter, G., *Luther, his Life and Work* (trans. J. Riches, 1963)

Rupp, E. G., *Luther's Progress to the Diet of Worms* (1951)

Rupp, E. G., *The Righteousness of God* (1953)

Schwiebert, E. G., *Luther and his Times* (St Louis, 1950)

Schwiebert, E. G., 'New Groups and Ideas at the University of Wittenberg' in *Archiv für Reformationsgeschichte*, XLIX (1958), 60–78

Watson, P. S., *Let God be God!* (1947)

THE RADICALS

Bainton, R. H., *Hunted Heretic; the Life and Death of Michael Servetus* (Boston, 1953)

Clasen, C. P., 'Medieval Heresies in the Reformation' in *Church History*, XXXII (1963), 392–414

Cohn, N., *The Pursuit of the Millennium* (1957)

Jones, R. M., *Spiritual Reformers in the 16th and 17th Centuries* (1914)

Hillerbrand, H. J., 'The Origin of Sixteenth Century Anabaptism' in *Archiv für Reformationsgeschichte*, LIII (1962), 152–80

Hillerbrand, H. J., 'Menno Simons' in *Church History*, XXXI (1962), 387–99

Kot, S., *Socinianism in Poland* (trans. E. M. Wilbur, Boston, 1957)

Maier, P. L., 'Caspar Schwenckfeld in' *Archiv für Reformationsgeschichte*, LIV (1963), 89–97

Rupp, E. G., 'Andrew Karlstadt and Reformation Puritanism' in *Journal of Theological Studies*, X (1959), 308–26

Rupp, E. G., 'Word and Spirit in the First Years of the Reformation' in *Archiv für Reformationsgeschichte*, XLIX (1958), 13–26

Rupp, E. G., 'Thomas Müntzer, Hans Huth and the Gospel of All Creatures' in *Bulletin of the John Rylands Library*, XLIII (1961), 492–519

Wilbur, E. M., *A History of Unitarianism, Socinianism and its Antecedents* (Boston, 1945)

Williams, G. H., *The Radical Reformation* (1962)

Williams, G. H. (ed.), *Spiritual and Anabaptist Writers* (Library of Christian Classics, XXV, 1957)

ZWINGLIANISM AND CALVINISM

Birnbaum, N., 'The Zwinglian Reformation in Zürich' in *Past and Present*, No. 15 (1959), 27–47

Donaldson, G., *The Scottish Reformation* (1960)

Fox, P., *The Reformation in Poland* (Baltimore, 1924)

Hall, B., *John Calvin* (Historical Association, G.33, 1956)

Hughes, P. E., 'The Geneva of John Calvin' in *The Churchman*, LXXVIII (1964), 254–75

Hunt, R. N. C., *John Calvin* (1933)

Kingdon, R. M., 'The Political Resistance of the Calvinists in France and the Low Countries' in *Church History*, XXVII (1958), 220–33

Koenigsberger, H. G., 'The Organization of Revolutionary Parties in France and the Netherlands during the Sixteenth Century' in *Journal of Modern History*, XXVII (1955), 335–51

McNeill, J. T., *The History and Character of Calvinism* (New York, 1954)

McNeill, J. T., 'Calvin as an Ecumenical Churchman' in *Church History*, XXXII (1963), 379–91

Potter, G. R., ch. vi–viii in E. Bonjour, H. S. Offler and G. R. Potter, *A Short History of Switzerland* (1952)

Schöffer, I., 'Protestantism in Flux during the Revolt of the Netherlands' in *Britain and the Netherlands*, II, ed. J. S. Bromley and E. H. Kossman (Groningen, 1964), 67–83

Wendel, F., *Calvin, The Origins and Development of his Religious Thought* (trans. P. Mairet, 1963)

ENGLAND

Bindoff, S. T., *Tudor England* (1950)

Clebsch, W. A., *England's Earliest Protestants 1520–1535* (New Haven and London, 1964)

Dickens, A. G., *The English Reformation* (1964, 1965)

Dugmore, C. W., *The Mass and the English Reformers* (1958)

Elton, G. R., *England under the Tudors* (1955)

Hill, C., *Economic Problems of the Church* (1956)

Hopf, C., *Martin Bucer and the English Reformation* (1946)

Hughes, P., *The Reformation in England* (3 vols., 1950–53–54)

Jordan, W. K., *The Development of Religious Toleration in England* (1932)

Knowles, D., *The Religious Orders in England*, III (1959)

Mozley, J. F., *Coverdale and his Bibles* (1953)

Neale, J. E., *Elizabeth I and her Parliaments, 1559–1581* (1953)

Parker, T. M., *The English Reformation to 1558* (1950)

Pollard, A. F., *Wolsey* (1929, 1953)

Pollard, A. F., *The Political History of England*, VI, 1547–1603 (1910)

Porter, H. C., *Reformation and Reaction in Tudor Cambridge* (1958)

Richardson, W. C., *History of the Court of Augmentations 1536–1554* (Baton Rouge, 1961)

Ridley, J., *Thomas Cranmer* (1962)

Rowse, A. L., *The England of Elizabeth* (1950)

Rupp, E. G., *Studies in the Making of the English Protestant Tradition* (1947)

Zeeveld, W. G., *Foundations of Tudor Policy* (Cambridge, Mass., 1948)

LIST OF ILLUSTRATIONS

86 Map of Switzerland in the sixteenth century. Drawn by Marc Sale

87 Zürich: painted view by Hans Leu the Elder, early sixteenth century. Schweizerisches Landesmuseum, Zürich

88 Zwingli by Hans Asper, 1531 or after. Kunstmuseum, Winterthur

89 Glarus: wood-cut view from Johannes Stumpf, *Chronik der Eydgenossen*, Zürich, 1548. British Museum

90 Fate of an indulgence-pedlar, from Niklaus Manuel Deutsch, *Ablasskrämer*, 1523. Stadtbibliothek, Berne

91 Pages from Luther's *Auslegung der Episteln und Evangelien*, Basle, 1522, with Zwingli's marginalia. Zwingli-Museum, Stadtbibliothek, Zürich

92 Swiss mercenaries at Einsiedeln: contemporary miniature from Diebold Schilling's *Luzerner Chronik*. Bürgerbibliothek, Lucerne: Photo Martin Hürlimann

93 Johannes Hussgen (Oecolampadius) of Basle: portrait from Theodore Beza, *Icones*, Geneva, 1580. British Museum

94 Title-page of Zwingli's *Von Göttlicher und Menschlicher Gerechtigheit*, printed by Christoph Froschauer, Zürich, 1523. British Museum

95 Heinrich Bullinger: anonymous painted portrait. Zwingli-Museum, Stadtbibliothek, Zürich

96 Swiss copy of the Marburg Protocol, 1529, last sheet. Staatsarchiv, Zürich

97 Hans Huth: portrait by C. van Sichem from his *Iconica*, Arnhem, 1609. British Museum

98 Title-page of Daniel Featley, *Description of the Severall Sorts of Anabaptists*, London, 1645/6. British Museum

99 A Hutterite family: from the title-page of C. Erhard, *Von Münsterschen Widertauffer*, Munich, 1589

100 Anti-Hutterite lampoon: from the title-page of *Der Hutterischen Widertauffer Taubenköbel*, Ingolstadt, 1607. British Museum

101 Bernhard Knipperdolling: engraved portrait by Heinrich Aldegrever, 1536. Courtauld Institute of Art, London

102 Melchior Hoffman: portrait by C. van Sichem, from *Het Tooneel der Hoofketteren*, Middleburgh, 1677. British Museum

103 Michael Servetus: portrait by C. van Sichem, from *Het Tooneel der Hoofketteren*, Middleburgh, 1677. British Museum

104 Jan Matthys: portrait by C. van Sichem, from *Het Tooneel der Hoofketteren*, Middleburgh, 1677. British Museum

105 John of Leydon: portrait by Heinrich Aldegrever, 1534–5. By courtesy of the Trustees of the British Museum

106 Siege of Münster: wood-cut by Erhard Schoen. British Museum

107 Torture-chamber: wood-cut by Hans Weiditz, from Petrarch, *Trostspiegel*, Augsburg, 1532. British Museum

108 Title-page of the Schleitheim Confession, 1527

109 Menno Simons: portrait by C. van Sichem, from *Het Tooneel der Hoofketteren*, Middleburgh, 1677. British Museum

110 Execution of Anabaptists in the Netherlands, 524: engraving from Tieleman Jans van Braght, *Het Bloedig Tooneel* ('The Bloody Theatre'), Amsterdam, 1685. British Museum

111 Title-page of the Old Testament Prophets in German, edited by Ludwig Haetzer and Hans Denck, Augsburg, 1527. British Museum

112 Title-page of Sebastian Franck, *Chronica, Zeitbuch und Geschichtbibel*, Strassburg, 1531. British Museum

113 Caspar Schwenckfeld: engraved portrait, 1556. British Museum

114 Calvin: anonymous painted portrait, about 1534. Musée Historique de la Réformation, Geneva: Photo Jean Arlaud

115 Panorama of Geneva by Claude Chastillon, engraved by Merian in 1650. British Museum

116 Martin Bucer: engraved portrait by René Boivin, 1544. British Museum

117 Guillaume Farel: anonymous painted portrait. Bibliothèque de la Ville, Neuchâtel

118 Title-page of Calvin, Institutio Christianae Religionis, Geneva, 1559. British Museum

119 Calvinist setting of Psalm CXXXVII, in the translation of Clément Marot

120 German satire on the Calvinist Lord's Supper: engraving by Johann Krell. From Emile Doumergue, Iconographie Calvinienne, Lausanne, 1909

121 The old Calvin: sketch by a student, about 1564. Bibliothèque Publique et Universitaire, Geneva

122 Theodore Beza: engraved portrait by J. Hogenberg, 1595

123 Anti-Huguenot lampoon, about 1632. From Emile Doumergue, Iconographie Calvinienne, Lausanne, 1909

124 Huguenots as apes, by G. de Saconay, from Généalogie et la Fin des Huguenaux, Lyon, 1573. From Emile Doumergue, Iconographie Calvinienne, Lausanne, 1909

125 Caricature of Calvin painted by Giuseppe Arcimboldi, 1566. Gripsholm: Photo Svenska Porträttarkivet, Stockholm

126 Iconoclasm in the Netherlands: engraving from Baron Eytzinger, De Leone Belgico, Cologne, 1583. British Museum

127 'Temple de Lyon, dit du Paradis': anonymous painting of 1564. Bibliothèque Publique et Universitaire, Geneva

128 St John the Baptist Preaching, by Brueghel. Budapest Museum

129 Hercules slaying the Hydra: a medal struck by order of Charles IX after the Massacre of St Bartholomew, 1572. Bibliothèque Nationale, Paris

130 'La Saint-Barthélémy', 1572: painting by François Dubois d'Amiens. Musée cantonal, Lausanne: Photo André Held

131 Spanish troops leaving Maastricht, 1577: engraving from Baron Eytzinger, De Leone Belgico, Cologne, 1583. British Museum

132 The Appellation of John Knox: title-page of an edition of 1644

133 John Knox: engraved portrait by Hondius. British Museum

134 Sigismund II Augustus and the Pope in coalition: engraving from Stanislaw Orzechowski, Quincunx, Cracow, 1564. British Museum

135 Stephen I Báthory: contemporary engraved portrait. Germanisches Nationalmuseum, Nuremberg

136 The burning of Bishops Latimer and Ridley, 1555: engraving from John Foxe, Actes and Monuments, London, 1563

137 Title-page of the Geneva Bible, 1560. British Museum

138 Title-page of Cranmer's Book of Common Prayer, London, 1549. British Museum

139 Map: the religious situation in central Europe about 1550, showing the approximate extent of the revolt from Rome. Drawn by Marc Sale

INDEX

Numbers in italics refer to illustrations

213